NAPOLEON 1812

NAPOLEON 1812

NIGEL NICOLSON

A Cornelia & Michael Bessie Book

HARPER & ROW, PUBLISHERS, New York
Cambridge, Philadelphia, San Francisco, London
Mexico City, São Paulo, Singapore, Sydney

This work was originally published in Great Britain by George Weidenfeld & Nicolson Limited.

NAPOLEON 1812. Copyright © 1985 by Nigel Nicolson. All rights reserved. Printed in the United States of America. No part of this book may be used or reproduced in any manner whatsoever without permission except in the case of brief quotations embodied in critical articles and reviews. For information address Harper & Row, Publishers, Inc., 10 East 53rd Street, New York, N.Y. 10022. Published simultaneously in Canada by Fitzhenry & Whiteside Limited, Toronto.

FIRST U.S. EDITION

Maps by Richard Natkiel

Library of Congress Cataloging-in-Publication Data

Nicolson, Nigel.
  Napoleon, 1812.

  "A Cornelia and Michael Bessie book."
  Bibliography: p.
  Includes index.
  1. Napoleonic Wars, 1800–1814—Campaigns—Soviet Union. 2. Napoleon, Emperor of the French, 1769–1821. I. Title.
DC235.N53   1985   940.2'7   82-48676
ISBN 0-06-039043-3

85 86 87 88 89 RRD 10 9 8 7 6 5 4 3 2 1

To Henry Anglesey

CONTENTS

ILLUSTRATIONS

SKETCH MAPS

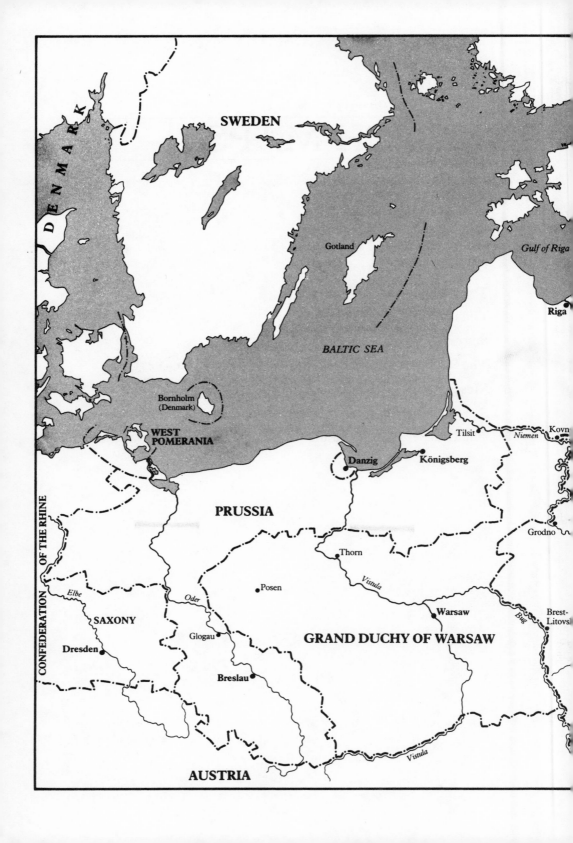

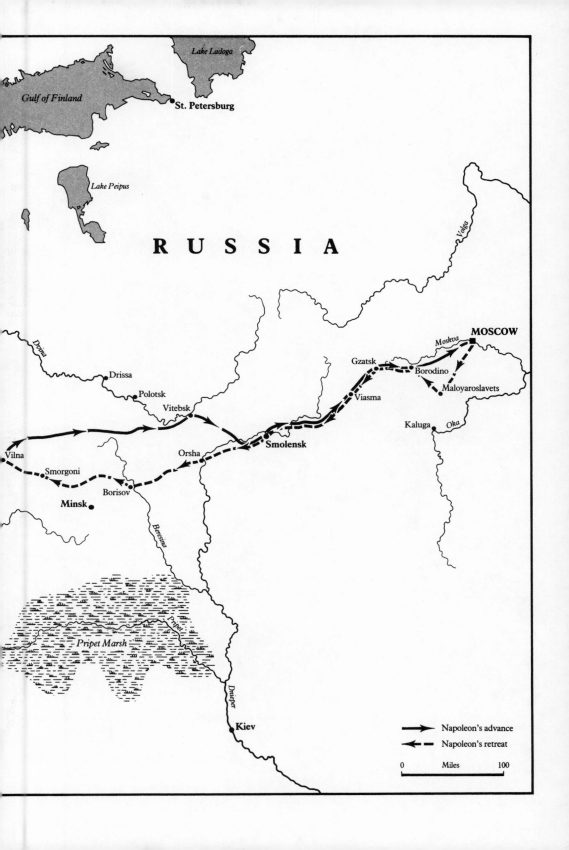

CHAPTER ONE

THE CAUSES
AND THE
PREPARATIONS

Once at St Helena, ruminating on a past for which there was no future, Napoleon said that he wished he had died in Moscow. 'Sire,' Las Cases replied, 'history would have been deprived of the return from Elba, the most heroic act any man has ever accomplished.' 'Well,' said the Emperor, who could tolerate flattery better than most men, 'I imagine there is something in that. But say Waterloo. That is where I should have died.'

In defeat? If a great commander yearns for death in battle in order to consummate his career, it should be at a Trafalgar, a Quebec. In fact St Helena, though humiliating and squalid as a place of internment, gave him time to dictate the memorial which has never ceased to irradiate his legend. His tomb of red Russian porphyry in the Invalides bears no name. No tourist needs to be told whose it is. Only one other tomb in all Europe, Columbus's in Seville Cathedral, is so moving to contemplate, and only one man in all French history deserves so splendid an anonymity. Around its base are carved the names of a dozen of his most famous battles, among them La Moskowa, known to all the world except the French as Borodino. In first choosing Moscow as the scene of his death, he probably meant this battle, named after its eponymous river, Moskva, but wrongly spelled, for in the city itself there was no fighting. He could have died there only by assassination, plague, or ignominiously in the fire.

However, there would have been a certain glory in it. Moscow marked the furthest limit of his conquests, more distant from Paris even than Acre in 1799, and he had reached it entirely by land. The Egyptian expedition had been accomplished mainly by sea, which to him was an unworthy shortcut. But what would history's verdict have been if he had died in Moscow? Not that his campaign was a brilliant failure, but that he had led an army to its destruction made more inevitable by his death. Of all the gambles implicit in it, the most risky was that he would not survive it. There was not a single Marshal who could replace him – not Murat, Davout, or even Ney. Moscow was in ruins, its supplies on the point of exhaustion, an undefeated enemy just outside it and growing daily in strength and confidence, the French communications under constant threat, and winter approaching. It would have been said that his death was an ignoble form of suicide, a fate deserved by a tyrant who had over-reached his grasp.

As it was, the Russian campaign, which occupied from beginning to end only six months, June to December 1812, added to the Napoleonic legend an episode on the grandest scale, and augments his stature because it was so audacious, and, paradoxically, because it ended in total failure. Though morally unjustifiable and strategically unsound, the campaign remains proof of his genius for resilience. The retreat exposed him to adversities which would have compelled the capitulation of any lesser general. He managed to control from these immense distances the politics and administration of a vast Empire. His escape from the encircling grasp of three converging Russian armies at the Beresina is one of the most dramatic achievements in military history. That he was able to return undaunted to Paris, leaving behind him the relics of a frozen, famished, but still loyal army, and was immediately able to raise a new one, was not seen then, and is not seen now, as a callous betrayal, but as the most striking evidence of his hold upon the hearts of his countrymen.

Few chapters in Napoleon's story are better documented. The vast contemporary archive of his letters and orders has long since been published. To take part in a campaign which afforded such opportunities for personal glory, and to have survived such immense dangers and hardships, induced men on both sides, from high commanders to sergeants, to record their experiences with a pride and wealth of detail that are unmatched in the records of Napoleon's other campaigns. A library of comment on the conduct of the war, to which this is one contribution, has never ceased to grow. One of the world's greatest novels was shaped around it, and Tchaikovsky's famous overture. Men like Ney and Kutuzov, Murat and Bagration, already renowned for their previous exploits, are best remembered for their achievements in 1812. So is Alexander I of Russia.

The hold which the campaign has upon our imaginations is due to its tragic evolution, its unity in space and time, the vicarious pleasure which most of us take in reading, from positions of comfort and security, of the ordeals and emotions of other men in situations of great peril, and in calculating, with the benefit of hindsight and the lack of any responsibility for what occurred, where things went wrong, on both sides. Tolstoy believed that Napoleon was bound to fail, that his influence on predestined events was negligible, and that the Russians succeeded because the tide of history demanded it. To us this mystic explanation seems inadequate. It is clear that certain events came about, not because they were inevitable, but because decisions were made by individuals acting from guesswork and their previous experience; that their characters (Napoleon's in wanting to press forwards, Kutuzov's in wanting to hold back) determined what they did; and that good luck and ill luck played alternate roles in their respective fortunes. The purpose of this narrative is not to add new facts to what is already known, but to examine the story afresh, consider why one of the greatest commanders in history failed and one of its least gifted succeeded, how Tolstoy misinterpreted the drama, and how Hitler, 130 years later, failed to benefit from Napoleon's example, just as Napoleon ignored, in spite of much study, the lesson of the disaster that overcame the Swedish king, Charles XII, a hundred years before him, when he too attempted to conquer the unconquerable. And to arouse speculation, admiration and sympathy, together with despair at the folly and wastage of it all.

Napoleon was forty-two when it began. He celebrated his next birthday on 15 August 1812 as he arrived at the outskirts of

3

Smolensk, the first major battle of the campaign. His age, and his unbroken success in war and politics, suggested to contemporaries, and to himself, that no achievement was beyond him. His belief in his invincibility, shared by his allies, his army and his opponents, was a major reason in determining him to strike at Russia. While his energy was undiminished he must dispose of the only continental power that remained a threat to him, before turning finally upon England. The physical and mental prowess that he displayed during 1812 seemed to justify his confidence. Only once, before and during the battle of Borodino, did he suffer from any disability, and he endured the hardships of the retreat with a stamina that was astounding, even if one allows for the special care taken of his diet and small comforts by his staff. True, his appearance was not that of a fit man. It was coarsening. He had become corpulent from over-eating. Never a great horseman, he found it wearying to ride for long periods. His hair was thinning, and his cheeks had a hint of flabbiness. He carried his massive head on almost neckless, hunched shoulders. But none of these signs of incipient middle age diminished the air of authority that he exuded. 'Great men', wrote Marguerite Yourcenar in her version of Hadrian's memoirs, 'are characterized precisely by the extreme position which they take, and their heroism consists in holding to that extremity throughout their lives.' So it was with Napoleon. His reputation, his unchallengeable position as Emperor, the quickness of his mind and decisions, the terror that he aroused or the hope of approval, made most men quake or fawn in his presence, and his familiarity with this reaction made him easily contemptuous. His light grey eyes were so piercing that few could hold his gaze. Men are seldom at their best when confronted by superior genius and power. 'Everyone', wrote Caulaincourt, who was one of the few who refused to be intimidated by him, 'complained of his manner of speaking to them. It was rarely that he exhibited the least appearance of kindliness, and when he showed that he was pleased, one might almost say that it was in spite of himself.' Stendhal noticed that his smile was theatrical. The teeth showed, but there was no corresponding expression in the eyes. When he wished, Caulaincourt remarked elsewhere, 'there could be a power of persuasion and fascination in his voice....

No woman was ever more artful than him in making you want, or agree to, his own desire.'

Though he lacked refinement of manner, he could be gracious, or give the appearance of it, as a necessary part of the regal manner he assumed. He had a low opinion of human nature, believing that self-interest was everyone's main motive, and prided himself on being able to extract the most from mediocre men. 'Probity, discretion and activity', he once said, 'are all that I demand of a man,' but he was flattering himself. What he demanded was not integrity but the strength to serve him. Only dreamers are interested in ethical qualities. With attractive women his attitude was at first unctuous, then lustful and possessive. Wishing to be thought a romantic, but in fact emotionally immature, and convincing himself that women found power the greatest of all aphrodisiacs, he could boast, even to his wife, of his conquests of the night before, sparing Josephine no detail of the lady's appearance and performance. Napoleon was not a civilized man. He was still a child of the Revolution, a man of unscrupulous ambition, a political and military genius of extraordinary skill, daring and determination, who could temporarily fake gentility and even charm, but a monster who could tell Metternich, as Hitler told his entourage, that if fortune turned against him, he would willingly drag down the whole of society in his fall.

To a man of such formidable personality, total concentration of command in his own person came naturally. He was Emperor and Generalissimo. He elevated his marshals to dukedoms, princedoms and even kingships, but did not trust them with responsibilities commensurate to their new rank, thus weakening not only their authority but their self-confidence. Berthier, his Chief-of-Staff, accepted a role little higher than that of amanuensis. Napoleon would check every detail of regimental strengths, promotion, supply, intelligence and medical services, as well as the disposition of his troops on a battlefield or the country leading to it. He was quick to anger, but exaggerated it for effect. So confident and insistent were his orders that few of his subordinates dared to ask for greater precision, let alone question them. He would complain of a lack of initiative when his authoritarian manner made it almost impossible, and of failures which were often due to his refusal to discuss his plans with those who had to execute them. He was a difficult man to serve, but such was his habit of success that the very issue of an order carried conviction that it was the right one. He gained immediate obedience, particularly in the most desperate circumstances when all depended upon his judgement. There were moments in the Russian campaign, as after the burning of Moscow and later at Maloyaroslavets, when he was uncertain enough to seek his Marshals' opinions, and he would often speculate in their company at great length on the options open to him, but it was in no sense a council-of-war. They waited on his decision, and then executed it with a zest and courage, and an absence of recrimination if things went wrong, that left no doubt that the loyalty on which he could draw was inexhaustible.

Marmont said, long after Napoleon's death, 'We marched surrounded by a kind of radiance whose warmth I can still feel as I did fifty years ago.' The humblest infantry soldier felt the same. Napoleon never needed to bully his men into obedience. He abolished flogging in the army. By his own example he held out the hope of glory as the supreme incentive, the honour of fighting under his command, the hope of earning from him, perhaps once in the course of a campaign, a nod of recognition after a battle, promotion by a rank, or an eagle for a battalion which had distinguished itself; and this devotion, augmented by his sublime remoteness from them, affected not only his own countrymen, but thousands of subject Poles, Germans and Italians. His paternalism was imitated, instinctively, by all his officers. The attachment between officer and man was most in evidence during the last phase of the retreat from Moscow, when soldiers would share their last piece of bread with their captain, and carry him for miles if he were wounded, and vice versa, in what one of the regimental commanders, Fezensac, called 'a reciprocity of care'. Discipline was rooted in trust and affection, and need never be severe. Tolerance was shown towards scavengers when they were hungry or looted a bauble to take back home. Never was morale more important than in this campaign. There were occasions when it collapsed, chiefly among stragglers who were deprived of the physical and moral support of coherent units, and brutality, even cannibalism, were not unknown. But the explanation why simple men endured so much without loading on their Emperor the reproaches he undoubtedly deserved, and why they faced, actually welcomed, desperate encounters with the enemy, when nobody would even notice how they died, was Napoleon's capacity to persuade them that this was the life, and death, that every worthy man would choose.

His leadership of men was his supreme gift. He inspired in his army an assumption of victory, and corresponding defeatism in his enemy. It was a more potent gift even than his tactical skill, for he was no great innovator in battle. Add to this his strategical sense of time-and-motion, his instinct for what his opponent would do, where they could be taken by surprise, his feeling for topography, river-lines and roads, forests, key-towns and prepared fortifications, which channel marching troops in certain directions, and his matchless capacity to organize the convergence of far-separated corps upon a certain spot at a certain time to gain him an advantage. This accumulation of talents, proved and refined during a period of fifteen years without a setback, combined with his extraordinary achievements in other fields – political, diplomatic, administrative, legal and in the arts – made Napoleon a figure of supernatural stature. Wellington never deviated from his opinion that his presence on a field of battle was worth 40,000 men, and when asked who was the greatest General of his age, replied, 'In this age, in past ages, in any age, Napoleon.'

There was, however, a penalty to be paid for his uninterrupted success. He became over-confident. Believing that nothing was beyond his grasp provided that he was personally in command, he assumed a burden that was too heavy even for him. His strength of will cut him off from his advisers. He convinced himself that he was sent by Providence to impose on half the world the rule and institutions of his own people, as Hitler also believed. His malign conceit would brook no rivals or equals. Shortly before he invaded Russia, he said to Fouché, his former Minister of Police, 'My destiny is not yet accomplished. The picture as yet exists only in outline. There must be one code, one court of appeal, and one coinage, for all Europe. The states of Europe must be melted into one nation, and Paris will be its capital.' At St Helena, speaking to O'Meara about his career, he attempted to justify his tyranny:

> I purified the Revolution, dignified nations and established kings.... At what point can I be assailed? Can it be for my intentions? But even here I can find absolution. Can it be for my despotism? It can be demonstrated that the Dictatorship was an absolute necessity. Will it be said that I restrained liberty? It can be proved that licentiousness, anarchy and the greatest irregularities still haunted the threshold of liberty. Shall I be accused of being too fond of war? It can be shown that I always received the first attack. Will it be said that I aimed at universal monarchy? It can be proved that this was the result of fortuitous circumstances, and that my enemies led me step by step to this determination. Lastly, shall I be blamed for my ambition? This passion I must doubtless be allowed to have possessed, and that in no small degree; but at the same time, my ambition was of the highest and noblest kind that ever perhaps existed – that of establishing and of consecrating the empire of reason, and the full exercise and complete enjoyment of all the human faculties. And here the historians will probably feel impelled to regret that such ambition should not have been fulfilled or gratified. This is my whole history in a few words.

In these 'few words' he puts fairly the accusations of which history holds him guilty, only to magnify them by his plea of innocence. He did not dignify nations, except by their resistance to him. He did not establish 'an empire of reason', but of force. He was not led by his enemies to aim for universal monarchy; he tried to impose it. He did not await the first attack; he was always the aggressor. In 1812 his motives were inexcusable, his pride self-destructive. The Russian campaign exposes the weakness of all tyranny, that it can command obedience but not assent, and that conquest requires further conquest, until the point is reached when an empire becomes top-heavy, and its component parts, individual nations resentful of their subjugation, await a crack in the structure to bring it down. Ségur put it like this: 'France had antagonized nations by its conquests, Kings by its Revolution and new dynasty. She could have neither friends or rivals, only subjects. The first would have proved false, the second implacable. So France needed that all should be subject to her, else she would be subject to them.'

A mental map of Europe at the height of Napoleon's power is a necessary preliminary to what follows. In 1799 he had become First Consul of France, in 1804 its Emperor. He defeated the Russian–Austrian army at Austerlitz in 1805, Prussia at Jena-Auerstadt in 1806, Russia at Friedland in 1807. Renewed hostilities with Austria led to their second defeat at Wagram in 1809. Switzerland was under French protection. North-east Italy, Naples and Westphalia were ruled by members of his family. The larger part of Poland was formed into the Grand Duchy of Warsaw under his control. Belgium, Holland, the Hanseatic coast of Germany and the Confederation of the Rhine were totally dependent upon his will. While Austria, Prussia and Russia were nominally allied to him, their cooperation depended upon his continued success. The only defiant enemy was Great Britain, dominant at sea since Trafalgar, but now engaged with him on land only in Spain and Portugal, where peasant revolts had led to Wellesley's invasion in 1808. We have a picture of western, southern and central Europe under the supreme control of a single man, whose military victories and their political exploitation were decisive in all but one quarter, Britain and her army in the Peninsula.

It was a situation curiously similar to that in 1940–41. Both Napoleon and Hitler controlled continental Europe. Neither could defeat Britain so long as she retained her mastery at sea, and for that reason both abandoned their projected invasion of the British Isles. But Britain could not hope to overcome her enemy without the help of major land-powers on the Continent. Spain in the 1800s was the equivalent to North Africa in the early 1940s, sideshows where alone the enemies grappled on land. Both dictators turned to a strategy of economic stranglehold of Britain, in the 1800s by attempting to close all European ports to British trade, in the 1940s by unlimited submarine warfare. In both wars the dictators invaded Russia to render her powerless so that they could turn all their strength against

Britain, and both campaigns had the opposite result, that Russia became a victorious ally who enabled Britain to survive. The analogy breaks down only in the attitude of the United States, in the first war a temporary enemy, in the second an incomparable ally.

Napoleon's true reason for attacking Russia was that he feared her and resented her rivalry; his declared reason was that she refused to cooperate fully in his strategy to starve and bankrupt Britain into submission. It was not a strategy that could have succeeded, and Russia's tepid cooperation was not a main reason for its failure. This requires some explanation.

Great Britain traditionally exported to Europe her textiles, her iron, and raw materials from her colonies, like coffee, cotton and sugar. She imported timber from the Baltic and corn from France itself. Napoleon's Berlin Decree of November 1806 tightened a blockade which had been nominally in force since 1793. In future there was to be no commerce at all between Britain and the Continent, and all British goods already in store in countries under French control were to be destroyed. Britain responded by Orders in Council which imposed a counter-blockade against France and her allies. At Tilsit (July 1807) Tsar Alexander I agreed with Napoleon that Russia would abandon her British ally and collaborate with him in blockading her. The Continental System, as Napoleon called it, was further tightened in December 1807 by the Second Milan Decree, which extended the ban on British trade to all ships, including neutrals, which touched at a British port and submitted to search by the Royal Navy. The consequence of these restrictions was to impose considerable hardship on Britain, but also to antagonize neutrals like the United States, French merchants, and Napoleon's own allies, particularly Russia, who saw in them a symbol of his tyranny. When his agents burned British goods without compensation, it was an intolerable loss to more than Britain. Unless the blockade could be made quickly effective, Napoleon was in danger of damaging his own cause as much as his enemy's.

At first the system seemed to be working. In Britain it created a severe crisis. Her exports in 1808 dropped by twenty per cent, and her grain imports fell to one-twentieth of those in the previous year, raising the price of bread beyond the reach of the poor. Unemployment mounted and bankruptcies multiplied. In partial compensation, Britain was able to expand her trade with the Americas, and found through Turkey an outlet into Europe beyond Napoleon's control. There was a vast amount of smuggling from and into continental ports like Heligoland, the Channel Islands and Salonika, and Napoleon was obliged to relax some of his decrees in response to complaints from his farmers and merchants, allowing even the export of French corn to Britain – which averted a serious threat of starvation, his main weapon. By 1810 over eighty per cent of British wheat imports was coming from the Continent. It should by now have become clear to him that England could never be forced to submit by these methods alone, but he remained convinced that the system could at least paralyse her, provided that it was enforced as universally as possible.

The resulting losses and privations aroused untold resentment throughout Europe, and among the hardest hit was Russia. She had imported from Britain mainly textiles, and exported flax, hemp and above all timber for the construction of naval and merchant ships. When this trade was halted after Tilsit, her Government lost customs revenue, her merchants a large part of their profits, and the nobility, who owned the majority of the forests, a main source of their income. As Russia could export nothing, she could import nothing, even essentials like sugar. Her adverse balance of trade prevented it. It became imperative for the Tsar to apply some remedy, in defiance of Napoleon. On the last day of 1810 he issued a ukase forbidding the import of luxury merchandise, including that of France itself, of which silk and wine were the most important, and at the same time admitted American and other neutral shipping to northern Russian harbours, thus circumventing the ban on their entry into neighbouring German ports. When the Emperor protested, Alexander replied that Napoleon himself had breached his system by allowing limited French exports to England and admitting neutral ships to his own harbours. 'Your Majesty', he wrote, 'cannot expect to impose on the Russians, as on the people of Hamburg, privations that you no longer impose on yourself.'

It was an entirely reasonable argument, but there were other causes of their worsening relationship. They were in competition for the acquisition of new territories. Since Tilsit, Alexander had subjugated Finland, which became semi-autonomous, with himself as Grand Duke, and he barely troubled to conceal his ambition to annex Constantinople and the Danubian province of Wallachia. He was at war with Turkey for this very purpose. The Tsar was deeply resentful of Napoleon's seizure in 1811 of the German coastal state of Oldenburg, whose Duke was married to the Tsar's sister, and suspected Napoleon of designing to enlarge the Duchy of Warsaw to create a new Polish kingdom; while Napoleon suspected Russia, which in 1796 had absorbed a large part of Poland, of planning to grab the rest. They were also in rivalry for the alliance of Sweden. All this manoeuvring at the expense of independent nations gave each of them good cause to distrust the other. The difference between them was that Napoleon believed that their quarrels could only be ended by war between them, while Alexander believed that they could be settled by compromise and fair exchange, and that this constant billowing of frontiers back and forth would eventually subside into an equilibrium. It has often been said that the Franco-Russian war of 1812 was inevitable. It was not. It broke out because one of the two Emperors desired it.

There was a more personal matter between them: Napoleon's second marriage. At their meeting at Erfurt in September 1808, Napoleon suggested to the Tsar through Talleyrand that he might cement the Tilsit alliance by divorcing Josephine, who had failed to give him a child, and marrying one of Alexander's sisters, of whom there were two, Catherine aged twenty and Anna not yet fifteen. His first choice was Catherine, but he was prepared to accept Anna. When Catherine married the Duke of Oldenburg, Napoleon made a formal request for Anna's hand. The idea was immediately scotched by the Dowager Empress, Alexander's and Anna's mother, who had the legal right to decide her daughter's future, ostensibly on religious grounds, but mainly because she regarded Napoleon with loathing and Tilsit as 'a pact with the devil'. The public excuse was that Anna was too young to marry. Napoleon must wait till she was eighteen. He took this, correctly, as a refusal. Looking elsewhere for a bride, he found Marie-Louise of Austria.

Of course his motive was dynastic and political. He could not feel secure without an heir. Josephine had had two children by her first marriage to Alexandre de Beauharnais, so it seemed that her barren condition as Napoleon's wife since 1796 might be due to his failing as a husband. However, Josephine was now forty-six, and his Polish mistress, Marie Walewska, bore him a son, and Eleonore Revel, the wife of a captain of dragoons, another child. There were perhaps others too. Napoleon still loved Josephine, but as he explained to her, 'in politics there is no heart, only head'. Though she fainted when told of his decision, in public she accepted it with dignity. Counsellor Pasquier wrote of her last appearance at a court function, where all the guests knew of her impending degradation, 'I could not help being struck by the perfection of her attitude. Only women can rise superior to the difficulties of such a situation, but I have my doubts whether a second one could be found to do it with such perfect grace and composure.' The divorce was allowed on the pretext that no parish priest had been present at their wedding, which was therefore invalid. She returned to Malmaison, where she lived until her death in May 1814, six weeks after Napoleon signed his first instrument of abdication.

Marie-Louise was the daughter of the Emperor Francis I of Austria and a great-niece of Marie-Antoinette. She was nineteen, modest, submissive to her father and husband, without political ambition, 'soft, good, innocent and fresh as a rose' as Napoleon said after their first nuptial night. He had never set eyes on her before their marriage, knowing her only by her portraits and favourable reports. The match was negotiated by Metternich, and the wedding took place in Vienna by proxy on 10 March 1810, his secretary Berthier standing in for the bridegroom. Napoleon eagerly awaited her at Compiègne (having tactfully removed from the palace walls paintings of his victories over the Austrians), and a few days later married her again in Notre Dame, where five Queens carried her train. On 20 March 1811 she bore him a son, whom he at once proclaimed King of Rome, in token of the Hapsburgs' boasted descent from the Caesars. After 1814 she refused to see Napoleon again, and he died not with her name on his lips, but Josephine's.

Alexander did not take the marriage as a personal affront. His family had, after all, received and refused Napoleon's first offer, and Napoleon had more reason to feel snubbed. But Alexander was not blind to its political consequences. It marked a further stage in their distancing. Austria was now doubly allied to France, and this had also been the motive of Francis I in giving away his daughter, on the urgent advice of Metternich, who argued that as Austria was not yet strong enough to challenge Napoleon again, she might as well 'substitute nuptials for hostility'. One of Napoleon's first actions after the marriage was to refuse to ratify his promise to Alexander not to revive an independent Poland, and the annexation of Oldenburg followed.

He believed (because he wanted to believe it) that Alexander was bent upon war with France, and might take the initiative. He made preparations to resist him by stationing huge bodies of troops in north-east Europe, from Danzig to Breslau, a move which increased Alexander's apprehension. It was a classic example of how fear of attack by each of two great powers provokes attack by one of them, and an ostensibly defensive stance slowly moves towards aggressive intent. From August 1811 Napoleon believed that an ultimate test of strength was bound to come, and he welcomed it. If France did not extend her power east, Russia would extend hers west. To Alexander the French Emperor now appeared the embodiment of evil, a creature of the Revolution, and it seemed to him that Russia might have been designed by Providence as the instrument of his overthrow. In this opinion he was encouraged by his nobles, and even by Talleyrand, who had treacherously whispered to Alexander at Erfurt phrases that have become famous: 'Sire, what are you doing here? You have to save Europe, and you will not succeed in doing so except by putting yourself in opposition to Napoleon. The French people are civilized, their Sovereign is not. The Sovereign of Russia is civilized, its people are not. It is therefore for the Sovereign of Russia to be the ally of the people of France.'

The fundamental difference between them, as Correlli Barnett has written, 'was that each man regarded himself as the greatest emperor in the world'. Napoleon imagined that at Tilsit Alexander had accepted second place (as Hitler thought of Mussolini after 1936), while Alexander believed that the expansion of the French Empire as far as his own borders would halt his own ambitions. In this he was not mistaken. The defeat of Russia would mean that the Baltic and Black Seas would be closed to commerce, and that Austria and Prussia would be too cowed to help him recover his position. If attacked, he would defend himself, but he dreaded the prospect. Napoleon thrived on it. The immensity of the task stimulated him. His abilities, and his army, were too great to waste on a mere consolidation of his Empire. All his reasons were excuses.

His capacity to deceive himself in deceiving others is best illustrated by his conversation with Caulaincourt on 5 June 1811, recorded by Caulaincourt in his memoirs from notes made at the time. General Armand Augustin Louis de Caulaincourt, Duke of Vicenza, had been sent to St Petersburg as Napoleon's Ambassador in 1807, and remained there four years. He became an intimate of the Tsar, admired him, and exerted his considerable charm and influence to maintain the Tilsit agreement in deed and spirit. His relationship with Napoleon was alternately sympathetic and uneasy. He was a man of great intelligence who never hesitated to speak his mind, and Napoleon responded, as powerful men do to subordinates whose honesty is greater than their fear. He claimed with justice that he had never been guilty of flattery, and to have 'touched up nothing and disguised nothing' in transcribing his daily notes for posterity. When accused by his master of being pro-Russian, he replied that he was 'proud to be against this war, to have done all I could to prevent it, but it was an outrage to doubt my fidelity and patriotism'. That has the ring of truth. Once during the course of the campaign, when he was goaded beyond endurance to offer his resignation, Napoleon easily talked him round. 'It was impossible to leave him,' wrote Caulaincourt. The proof of their mutual respect is that Napoleon chose him as his sole companion on his return to Paris after the collapse of the campaign.

Caulaincourt was recalled from St Petersburg in May 1811 at his own request ('another winter there is likely to kill me'), and reported to Napoleon at St Cloud on 5 June. The Emperor received him coldly, resentful of his despatches, which had constantly emphasized that Alexander wanted peace. On the contrary, Napoleon began, the Tsar was treacherous and arming for war against France. Caulaincourt replied that he had done nothing more than take precautions when he saw his frontier menaced by Napoleon's troop movements, and he was naturally alarmed by recent events in Poland and Oldenburg. At this, Napoleon lost his temper and told Caulaincourt that the Tsar had duped him. 'You believe that Russia does not want war, and that she would remain in the alliance and take steps to uphold the Continental System if I satisfy her as regards Poland?'

Caulaincourt replied that it was not only a matter of Poland, but of Napoleon's troop concentrations in Danzig and Prussia.

'They are afraid, then?'

'No, Sire. But being reasonable people, they prefer an open state of war to a situation which is not genuine peace.'

'So they think they can dictate to me?'

'No, Sire.'

'Nevertheless, if they insist on my evacuating Danzig just to gratify Alexander, that amounts to dictation.... Before long shall be in the position of having to ask Alexander's leave to hold a parade at Mayence! ... They believe that they can lead me on a string like that King of Poland. I am not Louis xv. The French people would not tolerate such a humiliation. They want to make war on me, I tell you.'

They then turned to Napoleon's running grievance that Russia had breached the Continental System. Caulaincourt argued that Russia had fully adhered to her side of the agreement made at Tilsit, but Napoleon himself had broken it by licensing French ships to trade with England.

'The Emperor smiled and pinched my ear, saying to me as he did so, "Are you really so fond of Alexander?" "No, Sire, but I am fond of peace."' He asked permission to give the Emperor his advice.

'Go on.'

'I see only two possible lines of conduct: to re-establish Poland, and proclaim her independence, thus getting the Poles on your side; or to maintain the Russian alliance, thus bringing about peace with England and settling your affairs in Spain.'

'Which line would you take?'

'Maintain the alliance, Sire. It is the more prudent course, and the one more likely to lead to peace.'

'You are always talking about peace. Peace is only worth having when it is lasting and honourable.'

Napoleon then repeated that Alexander was afraid of him, and Caulaincourt replied, in the most significant statement of the interview. 'No, Sire, because while recognizing your military talent, he has often pointed out to me that his country was large; that though your genius would give you many advantages over his generals, even if no occasion arose to fight you in advantageous circumstances, there was plenty of margin for ceding you territory, and that to separate you from France and from your resources would be, in itself, a means of successfully fighting you. "It will not be a one-day war," the Tsar Alexander said. Your Majesty will be obliged to return to France, and then every advantage will be with the Russians. Then the winter, the cruel climate, and most important of all, the Tsar's determination and avowed intention to prolong the struggle, and not, like so many monarchs, to have the weakness to sign a peace treaty in his capital.... Those are the very words, the thoughts, of the Tsar Alexander which I quote to Your Majesty.'

'Admit frankly', was Napoleon's only reply, 'that it is Alexander who wants to make war on me.'

'No, Sire, I would stake my life on him not firing the first shot or being the first to cross his frontiers.'

Thinking that Napoleon had not taken in the seriousness of the Tsar's warning, Caulaincourt strengthened it by quoting Alexander's parting words to him: 'It is possible, even probable, that we shall be defeated, but that does not mean that he will be able to dictate a peace. I shall not be the first to draw my sword, but I shall be the last to sheathe it. People don't know how to suffer. If the fighting went against me, I should retire to Kamtchatka rather than cede provinces and sign treaties in my capital that were really only truces. Your Frenchman is brave; but long privations and a bad climate wear him down and discourage him. Our climate, our winter, will fight on our side. With you, marvels only take place when the Emperor is in personal attendance; and he cannot be everywhere, he cannot be absent from Paris year after year.'

At this Napoleon fell temporarily silent, and Caulaincourt believed that the Tsar's reported words had made some impression on him, until he began to enumerate his own strengths, telling Caulaincourt that 'one good battle will knock the bottoms out of my friend Alexander's fine resolutions. He is fickle and feeble.' And then: 'It is the Austrian marriage that has set us at variance. The Tsar was angry because I did not marry his sister.'

Caulaincourt indicated that this was a travesty of the truth. 'It is for you, Sire, to decide whether there is to be peace or war. May I beseech Your Majesty, when you make your choice between the certain good of the one and the hazards of the other, to take full account of your own welfare and of the welfare of France.'

'You speak like a Russian.'

'On the contrary, like a good Frenchman, like one of Your Majesty's most faithful servants.'

They reverted finally to the Polish question, Caulaincourt pointing out that the Poles did not particularly wish to be 'liberated' by Napoleon. It was all too well understood in Europe that when he concerned himself with the affairs of a country, it was to serve his own rather than its interests.

'You think so, do you?'

'Yes, Sire.'

They then went in to dinner. Thus ended a conversation that had lasted five hours. It left Caulaincourt with no hope that peace would be maintained.

Ten weeks later, on 15 August 1811, at a reception in the Tuileries to celebrate his forty-second birthday, Napoleon approached the Russian Ambassador, Prince Kurakin, and in the hearing of everyone, complained that the Tsar wished to attack him. All the old grievances were reiterated – that Alexander was admitting neutral ships, that he had banned French imports, that he was moving troops to his frontier, that he was virtually ending their alliance. He didn't want war, but if it were forced upon him, he would win because he was stronger, and because he had always won. 'You count on allies, but where are they? Surely not Austria, from whom you have seized 300,000 souls in Galicia. Nor Prussia, which will surely remember Alexander's seizure of the Bialystok district. Nor Sweden, which will recall that you have reduced her to half her size by seizing Finland. All these injuries will be remembered, all these humiliations avenged. The entire Continent will be against you.'

The courtiers and Ambassadors listened to this aghast.

It was about this time that Napoleon took aside one of his ministers, thought to be Lacuée de Cessac, Minister of War, and told him that he had decided upon a great expedition, not naming its purpose, but saying that it would start by crossing the River Niemen on the Russian frontier. He would need horses and transport on the largest scale, 'because I intend to act over long distances and in different directions'. When the campaign was over, there would be 'years of peace and prosperity for us and our children after all these years of weariness and discomfort, but years also of glory'. De Cessac was to get busy at once.

While his military preparations went ahead, Napoleon also took diplomatic steps to ensure that his alliances were firm. The most important were those with Prussia and Austria, both defeated by him in war but still nominally independent. Both were required to mobilize troops for his expedition. Prussia signed a military alliance with France in February 1812. Its King, Frederick William III, after his defeat at Jena and the vivisection of his country at Tilsit, was terrified of Napoleon, who, he complained, treated him like a sergeant. If he did not comply with Napoleon's wishes, Berlin would be occupied by the French. He now agreed to supply an auxiliary corps of 20,000 men and provide the Grand Army with stores in enormous quantities, receiving in return some vague promises of 'territorial rewards' once the campaign had been successfully concluded.

Austria was more wary, but Metternich persuaded his Emperor that they had little choice, given that Napoleon already had 200,000 troops on their northern frontier. He might be so weakened by the forthcoming war that Austria could realign herself according to circumstances. So in March 1812 she concluded with France a military pact, promising to put at his disposal 30,000 men to act on the right wing of the army under the command of Prince Schwarzenberg, who had been Austrian Ambassador both in St Petersburg and in Paris. The bribe was that Napoleon would return to Austria her Illyrian provinces, ceded to him in 1809. Although secret, the pact soon became known to the Tsar, who took some consolation from Metternich's hint in May that Austria would not take her role very seriously, nor advance very deep into Russian territory, as indeed proved to be the case. The manoeuvre was subtle, and if one considers that the prime function of statesmanship is to protect the state, it did not lack a certain grandeur. At small cost Metternich had guaranteed Austria against invasion by either side.

Napoleon's centre was now firm, but he had not reckoned with the weakening of his northern and southern flanks. In March 1812, Sweden, under Bernadotte, his ex-marshal, signed a treaty of non-belligerent alliance with Russia in response to Napoleon's seizure of Swedish Pomerania (another weak link in the Continental System), and with his eye on annexing Norway with British and Russian connivance. Bernadotte had learnt from both Napoleon and Alexander how to capture and swap countries like pieces on a chess-board. Bernadotte did not intend to join either side, but his benevolent neutrality was more benevolent to Alexander than to his former Emperor. More harmful to Napoleon's prospects was the sudden signature on 28 May 1812 of peace between Russia and Turkey, for it released an experienced Russian army to oppose his invasion in the south. There was no certainty that Turkey would watch developments peacefully, so Napoleon was about to begin his campaign with doubtful neutrals on either side of it; but he considered that the rapidity of his advance would so astonish both of them that they would be no embarrassment to him, and that with his victory they would both fall under his control, thus completing the ring of ports closed to Britain. The two treaties were of greater importance to Alexander, who was relieved of anxiety on two fronts and considered with some reason that he had won the first round.

Although the evidence of his preparations left little doubt of his intentions, Napoleon was still pretending in the spring of 1812, even to his closest associates, that he did not want war with Russia. When Caulaincourt asked him why in that case he was assembling so vast an army in Prussia and Poland, when he needed the troops for Spain, he explained that his measures were purely precautionary, and tweaked his ear and cuffed the nape of his neck, always a sign of his good humour. In no way persuaded, Caulaincourt warned him that the frontiers of France were already too far-flung, and that his passion for conquering other countries would sooner or later end in tragedy. Napoleon laughed at what he called his friend's philanthropy. Pressing the point, Caulaincourt suggested that the strategy of blockade was far less likely to induce England to make peace than if he gave them some hope of a tranquil future by 'refashioning the States of Europe within reasonable boundaries'. The Emperor turned his back on him, saying that he understood nothing about policy. Just before Napoleon left Paris for the front, Caulaincourt tried again. He argued the risks of a Russian campaign, and the burden it would impose upon the youth of France. Napoleon replied shortly that Caulaincourt was misled by false reports. Russia was intending war. He must strike first.

Some public excuse must be given, and it was provided in response to a Russian note which Kurakin delivered to Napoleon on 27 April. Alexander undertook to withdraw his protest about the annexation .of Oldenburg, modify his ban on the import of French luxury goods, and reimpose the blockade on English ships, provided that Napoleon withdrew his troops from Prussia, as he had promised at Tilsit. Napoleon chose to regard this offer as an ultimatum, declaring that it proved what he had always suspected, that Alexander intended to invade and annex Prussia.

On 9 May 1812 he left St Cloud with Marie-Louise, and took the road to Dresden. He was in the highest spirits.

CHAPTER TWO

THE BEGINNING

The imperial journey to Dresden resembled a carnival. Three hundred new carriages had been ordered by senior officers from Paris coach-builders. Besides the military escort, it was a court on wheels, pages for the Emperor and maids-of-honour for Marie-Louise, and innumerable carts to carry plate and tapestries to set a brilliant scene in Dresden. They travelled briskly, the roads having been specially repaired ahead of them, crossing the Rhine at Mayence (Mainz) three days after leaving Paris, then Würzburg (13 May), Bayreuth (the 14th), and on the 15th they were met at Freyberg by the King of Saxony, who escorted them to Dresden, his capital, where they arrived shortly before midnight on 16 May, having completed a journey of 650 miles in a week.

Everywhere in Germany they had been greeted by princes who were honoured to put their palaces at Napoleon's disposal, even for an hour's rest. The common people at the roadside held up their children to set eyes on this famous man. At the entrance to Dresden a rainbow of coloured lanterns spanned the Elbe, and a torchlit procession led him to the palace of the Saxon King, who humbly vacated it for the fortnight of Napoleon's stay.

At St Helena he said that it was the grandest moment of his life, when every Sovereign in Europe except the Sultan, the Tsar and the King of England were at his feet. The Emperor Francis of Austria was there to greet his son-in-law; the King of Prussia ('merely a drill-sergeant, a blockhead', declared Napoleon, who allowed him only half-an-hour's audience); the King of Westphalia (Jerome, Napoleon's brother); the King of Bavaria, and all the minor princes and dukes of the Confederation of the

Rhine. There were formal receptions, ceremonial banquets, Masses in the Cathedral, an opera, a boar-hunt. Night after night an orchestra played softly in the saloons, while the people gathered outside to gaze upwards at the windows. Napoleon behaved with courtly affability, and deigned to ride once or twice through the streets. But his welcome, though ostentatiously, obsequiously, subservient at his levées, audiences and receptions, was not universal among the crowds. A boy, Wilhelm von Kügelgen, then nine years old, recalled in later life that his mother was told that if she came to the window, she could see Napoleon, who was about to pass. She replied, 'I shall withdraw to the kitchen, because I have little inclination to see the man who is in the process of crushing a poor nation [Russia] which has done him no harm.'

Everyone knew why Napoleon was there, though it was not mentioned in his presence. Implicitly, he was proclaiming a European war against barbarians, and the purpose of this extravagant display of his power was to frighten Alexander into submission, or provoke him to dare resistance. He had sent his aide-de-camp, Count Narbonne, to 'negotiate' with the Tsar at Vilna, which meant to deliver a final warning. Alexander received him courteously on 18 May and asked him what Napoleon wanted. 'Does he want to get me on his side, to compel me to adopt measures which will ruin my people? And because I refuse, he means to make war on me, in the belief that after two or three battles and the occupation of several provinces, I shall sue for peace, on terms dictated by himself. He is mistaken.' Then, unrolling a huge map, he went on: 'I am convinced that Napoleon is the greatest general in Europe, his armies are the best trained, his lieutenants the most courageous and experienced. But space is a barrier,' tapping the map, 'and if, after several defeats, I withdraw, sweeping the inhabitants along with me, if I let time, deserts and climate defend Russia for me, then perhaps I shall have the last word.' It was the same undaunted reply that he had given to Caulaincourt a year before, adding one new element, his threat to devastate and depopulate his country as fast as Napoleon advanced through it. He repeated that he would not be the first to draw the sword, and though he had no agreement with England, he would make one as soon as the first shot was fired. Next day he made it known to Narbonne that he had nothing further to say to him, sending three officers of his suite to pay him a farewell visit, and give him wines and provisions for his journey. When Narbonne reported to the Emperor in Dresden, Napoleon only replied, 'There is no more time to be lost in fruitless negotiations.' He left Dresden at 4 am on 29 May.

The second part of his journey was less splendid than the first. The Empress returned to Paris. Napoleon travelled fast in a covered carriage drawn by six horses, followed by Caulaincourt and Duroc in another. Their rate of progress averaged seven miles an hour over increasingly bad roads, and on this first day they pressed on for twenty hours with scarcely a halt to reach Glogau on the Oder. At Posen they stayed two days, at Thorn three, and on 7 June, after driving all day and night, they came to Danzig, Napoleon's main base, where Murat and Davout joined him, and he spent two weeks inspecting his troops there and at Königsberg, Insterburg and Gumbinnen, and organizing his administration. On 23 June he was on the Russian frontier, the River Niemen. He had come 1,200 miles from Paris. To Moscow it was another 500.

His demeanour during these anxious days was phlegmatic and solemn. He seldom responded to the acclamations of his troops except by a nod of approval. Now and again he would acknowledge the respectful greetings of the crowds, predominantly women, by raising his hat but without looking in their direction. The poet Heine, then fifteen years old, who watched him as he inspected the Guard at Thorn, wrote of the 'eternal eyes set in the marble of that imperial visage, looking on with the calm of destiny as his Guards marched past. He was sending them to Russia, and the old Grenadiers glanced up at him with an awesome devotion, a sympathetic earnestness, with the pride of death.' That night he was heard pacing up and down in the privacy of his bed-chamber singing the revolutionary song:

Et du nord au midi la trompette guerrière
A sonné l'heure des combats.
Tremblez, ennemis de la France.

It was not only the enemy that trembled. His allies, or those Prussians and Poles who lived in the vast region where his army was converging, suffered atrociously at the hands of troops who behaved as if they were already on hostile territory, looting, burning, raping and even killing those who resisted. Orders had been given to commandeer grain, brandy, cattle and transport from every billet they occupied for a night on their march to the frontier. Sometimes the owner was induced to accompany his horse and cart by the promise that he could return with them later, only to be dismissed after 100 kilometres without either. Rye was stripped from the fields, thatch from cottage roofs, to feed the animals. Untouched crops were trampled down by the never-ending echelons of infantry and cavalry. Occasionally the soldiers promised payment, but honoured only a tithe of it, believing that as they were on their way to war, they had the right to behave as conquerors. Protests were met with the sneer that the greatness of the expedition was worth the suffering of 400,000 peasants. The poverty of the Polish people, the sight of their stony fields and wretched cabins in contrast to those they had passed in Prussia, did nothing to arouse the army's pity. Not only the common soldier was guilty of such callousness. Emma, Lady Brownlow, tells in her memoirs that when the Allies entered Paris in 1813, a young Prussian officer was billetted in the house of an elderly French couple. They received him kindly, but before he left, he wrecked all the furniture in his bedroom. When asked why he had treated them so cruelly, he replied, 'I asked to be quartered in your house that I might let you see in one room what your son did to every room in my father's house in Berlin.' Before the campaign had even started, Napoleon, who did little to check these excesses and seemed indifferent to them, left behind him a morass of resentment which he came to regret later when he called for reinforcements from the two friendly countries which his men had ravaged.

Except in Spain, where Massena commanded 350,000 troops, there had been comparative peace in Europe since 1809, and Napoleon had been able to raise for his Russian campaign the largest army ever mobilized until that date, about 675,000 men, including the reserves, supply and garrison troops. Less than half of them were French. The others were willing, or less willing, allied and subject peoples – 40,000 Italians, who had marched all the way from Piedmont, Tuscany and Naples to East Prussia, Swiss, Dutch, some 30,000 Portuguese and Spaniards, Illyrians, Croats, Lithuanians and Germans from the Confederation of the Rhine and the Hanseatic states. All were incorporated into French formations, sometimes by brigades, sometimes in units as small as a battalion; but one Corps, the largest foreign contingent, was almost entirely Polish, another Prussian, another Saxon, and a fourth Austrian. The élite of the army was the Imperial Guard, composed of the Old and the Young Guard, in all nearly 50,000 men, and it remained under Napoleon's direct command. The order-of-battle can best be represented diagrammatically (opposite), using as a basis David Chandler's monumental Appendix G of his *Campaigns of Napoleon*, to introduce the main commanders and the size and nationality of their commands. To these must be added 18,000 engineers and administrative troops, and 157,000 men who garrisoned the towns or joined the Grand Army at intervals. Chandler makes the total 675,500 men, of whom about 500,000 actually entered Russia, taking with them over a thousand cannon. East of the Oder remained 226,000 men under arms. In France there were only 80,000 and in Spain 350,000.

As the Grand Army edged slowly towards the Niemen, morale was high. To the young French officers it was the most glorious and perhaps the last of Napoleon's adventures. It gave them a final opportunity for distinction and promotion. The hugeness of the country ahead did not dismay them. There was even talk of extending the campaign overland to conquer India. It was rumoured (and the rumour was true) that in the headquarter baggage were maps of Turkey, Central Asia and the Punjab. Captain Fantin des Odoards expressed the general emotion: 'The army has never shown itself more impatient to run after fresh triumphs. Its august leader has so accustomed it to fatigues, danger and glory that a state of repose would be hateful.' It was the same with many of the allied troops. Large numbers of them were mercenaries at heart, eager to ply their grisly trade under any command, against any enemy; and as a reward for their courage, there would be loot. The Poles and Lithuanians may

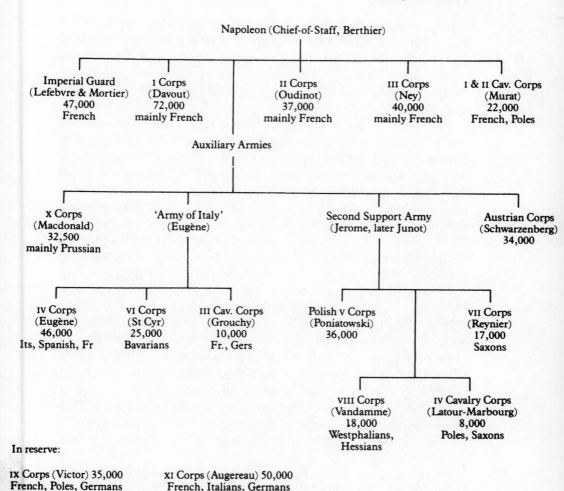

Napoleon (Chief-of-Staff, Berthier)

Imperial Guard
(Lefebvre & Mortier)
47,000
French

I Corps
(Davout)
72,000
mainly French

II Corps
(Oudinot)
37,000
mainly French

III Corps
(Ney)
40,000
mainly French

I & II Cav. Corps
(Murat)
22,000
French, Poles

Auxiliary Armies

X Corps
(Macdonald)
32,500
mainly Prussian

'Army of Italy'
(Eugène)

Second Support Army
(Jerome, later Junot)

Austrian Corps
(Schwarzenberg)
34,000

IV Corps
(Eugène)
46,000
Its, Spanish, Fr

VI Corps
(St Cyr)
25,000
Bavarians

III Cav. Corps
(Grouchy)
10,000
Fr., Gers

Polish V Corps
(Poniatowski)
36,000

VII Corps
(Reynier)
17,000
Saxons

VIII Corps
(Vandamme)
18,000
Westphalians,
Hessians

IV Cavalry Corps
(Latour-Marbourg)
8,000
Poles, Saxons

In reserve:

IX Corps (Victor) 35,000
French, Poles, Germans

XI Corps (Augereau) 50,000
French, Italians, Germans

have thought of it as a war to liberate their countries. Others had joined up only because they were obliged to do so. The Italians, for goodness knows what reasons, performed well, especially at Maloyaroslavets. The Spaniards and Dutch were the most unreliable, and desertions from their ranks began early. It was mercilessly suppressed. Tarlé records that when a group of 130 Spaniards were recaptured, the French colonel distributed tickets at random among them, half black, half white. Those with black tickets were shot.

Napoleon had had time to plan his strategy long before he left Paris. He had examined the maps, read all the accounts of Russia and its people that his librarian could supply, studied previous campaigns in Russia, and gathered from his envoys and spies detailed intelligence about the Tsar's armies, their commanders and dispositions.

The Russian army was smaller and less competent than his, but it had advantages that his did not – national homogeneity, familiarity with its own terrain, equipment more suited to summer and winter warfare, and a passionate determination which the invader, with his weaker motive, was unlikely to match when the going became tough. Accustomed to fighting Turks who took no prisoners, the rank-and-file would die rather than surrender. Their upbringing as serfs had disciplined them to endure extreme hardships. They were physically strong, ferocious but obedient to their officers, devoted to generals like Bagration and Kutuzov and reverential to the Tsar, religious, docile, childlike, possessing, as Sir Robert Wilson, who knew them well, remarked, 'all the energetic characteristics of a barbarian people, with the advantages grafted by civilization'. The cavalry were even better horsed than the French, and their artillery was at least equal, and expertly handled. The administration was poor by French standards, and the staffs ill-trained, but the advantage of operating on interior lines more than compensated for their shortcomings. At no stage of the campaign was there any threat to their main lines of communication, while Napoleon's were always in danger of being cut.

In the Cossacks the Russians had an arm which Napoleon lacked but badly needed in order to parry it. These were men mainly from the Crimea, Don and Volga regions, the bravest of the brave, the hardiest of the hardy, mounted on small, sturdy horses and armed with sabres, pistols and eight-foot lances. They were primarily skirmishers, adept at night-raids and at cutting off stragglers and foraging-parties, but they could combine, as at Borodino, in massed attacks. Brilliant horsemen, 'they could twist and turn their course through the most intricate country at full speed' (Wilson again). Their weaving tactics wore out their opponents by posing the constant threat of a swarming attack, from which they would withdraw as swiftly as they arrived. Like the Foreign Legion or the Gurkhas, their skill and their savage, reckless courage inspired great fear, and obliged the French to remain in tight formations in daytime and to stay sleepless on the alert at night.

In June 1812 Alexander had about 218,000 men deployed to oppose Napoleon's half-million. They were organized in three armies under the overall command of the Tsar. Their order-of-battle (borrowing Chandler's figures again) can be set out in shorter form than the French.

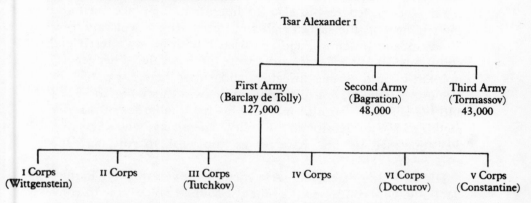

In addition there were, at the start, some 15,000 Cossacks, and the Army of the Danube under Chichagov, released from fighting the Turks by the Peace of Bucharest, but unable to march north in time to play much part until Napoleon had begun his retreat. In the rear, the Tsar's reserves were almost unlimited. Immediately available in the second line he had another 45,000 men, and behind them in distant garrisons a further 150,000. Militia levies were raised as fast as the campaign progressed. In short, at the beginning the Russians were outnumbered by three to one except in artillery, but as Napoleon's losses and detachments grew, and Russian reinforcements joined, the numbers slowly equalized, until at Borodino, only two and a half months later, they had achieved virtual parity. From then onwards Russian strength gained the ascendancy.

The Tsar was supreme commander. His power was not absolute, because his military inexperience made him dependent upon advisers, and his nobles could exert pressure on him, checking his more liberal ideas, like his proposal to introduce

29

income tax, give political rights to Jews and lift the more oppressive burdens from the serfs. His reforming zeal petered out. In foreign affairs he was no weakling, as his wars against Finland and Turkey had shown, and the admiration he had felt for Napoleon at Tilsit slowly turned to distrust and then hatred. He was called a vacillator, but Napoleon's contemptuous dismissal of him as 'a shifty Byzantine' was undeserved. His strength of will in a crisis could be adamantine. His inspiration was idealistic, almost mystic. He proclaimed his mission to be not only the defence of Russia but also the liberation of France itself and the triumph of 'the sacred rights of humanity', a declaration far in advance of his times, and at variance with his own territorial ambitions and the autocratic nature of his rule. The general opinion of him among his allies and subordinates was that he was unpredictable, not fully mature (he was thirty-five in 1812), and his chubby, youthful face and his habitual grace of manner increased the impression of fallibility. Speransky, who knew him well, summed up his character as 'too weak to rule, and too strong to be ruled'.

His two senior generals were men of proven quality. Barclay de Tolly, who combined the office of Minister of War with command of the First Army, owed his unexpected name to Scotch ancestry, but his family had emigrated to Livonia in the seventeenth century and he enlisted in the Russian army as a private soldier. He rose to high command after Eylau (1807), where he was gravely wounded, commanded brilliantly against the Swedes in Finland, and as Minister of War since 1810 had done much to modernize the army. He was respected but never aroused devotion, partly because of his non-Russian origins, and because he was outshone in character and ability by Bagration, who disliked and mistrusted him, and never concealed it. Prince Bagration was a Georgian of aristocratic lineage. He had fought at Austerlitz, Eylau and Friedland with a courage that became legendary. His temper when annoyed was uncontrollable, rendered all the more formidable by his strong, dark features and 'eyes flashing with Asiatic fire' (Sir Robert Wilson), but normally he was gentle, courteous and taciturn. To serve on his staff was regarded as a high honour, but extremely dangerous. He was the sort of man for whom the humblest soldier would willingly die.

Thus the battle-lines were drawn. It remains to describe the geography and the strategy, which to a large extent was determined by it.

The topography of Russia was quite well known to Europeans. (In *Mansfield Park*, written in the year of the invasion, the Bertram sisters sneer at their cousin Fanny Price, who, among other proofs of her ignorance, 'cannot tell the principal rivers of Russia'). Napoleon had maps printed in Paris on the scale of 1:500,000 which correctly positioned all the rivers, towns and main villages (Borodino, for example, but not Studenka on the Beresina), but did not show the forests and marshes, and marked all the roads as if they were equally viable. The Russian frontier lay along the Niemen and the Bug. Beyond lay generally level ground all the way to the Urals, but it was locally broken by wooded ravines and small undulations, and the cultivated lands were separated by vast swampy forests of birch and pine which effectively canalized traffic along tracks which often took two days' marching to traverse before re-emerging into open country. These tracks were unmetalled, laid on sandy soil or clay, dusty in hot weather, boggy after rain, and slippery in frost.

There was one major obstacle, the Pripet Marsh, a huge area of swamped woodland between Brest and Kiev, 150 miles north to south and 300 miles in width, crossed by only three causeway roads in poor condition. Its existence worked to Napoleon's advantage, for it confined the campaign to the country north of it, and sited his communications through Poland and Prussia, more reliably than through Austria. He was further helped by the directions of the main rivers. The watershed between the Dnieper, which flowed south to the Black Sea, and the Dvina, which flowed north to the Baltic, left a gap, 'the Orsha land-bridge', which led direct to Moscow. It was interrupted by a single river, the Beresina, a tributary of the Dnieper, which could be by-passed above its headwaters on the way to Vitebsk. Beyond, the river Moskva, which ran through Moscow itself, and the Oka, south of it, flowed conveniently parallel to the direction of the advance. Thus there was no major water-barrier which need impede Napoleon if he followed the natural lie of firm ground, and if obliged to bridge a major river, as he did the Dnieper, his engineers were capable of it.

His plan was to cross the Niemen with his main forces on quite a narrow front between Kovno and Grodno, and split Barclay's army in the north from Bagration's in the south, cutting their communications with St Petersburg, the capital. His flanks were to be protected by Macdonald's Corps advancing on Riga, and Schwarzenberg's Austrian Corps on Minsk. If Bagration took the offensive and aimed for Warsaw, he would be cut off. It was a classic Napoleonic strategy. Divide the enemy, defeat each part in detail, and keep the centre concentrated in order to advance well beyond the point where either could recover. The whole campaign might be over in six weeks.

It was much the same strategy as the Germans adopted in 1941, though they advanced deeper and on a wider front, with three million troops. While Napoleon's entire front was about 250 miles, the Germans were bound to extend theirs from northern Finland to the Black Sea, a distance of 1,300 miles, which widened, as they advanced, to 2,000. They foresaw a penetration as far east as Gorki, 1,000 miles from their starting-point, before a Russian capitulation could be expected. Their main thrust, like Napoleon's, was directed north of the Pripet Marsh across the Orsha land-bridge towards Moscow, and their intention, like his, was to encircle and destroy the Russian armies close to the frontier, so that the remainder of the campaign would be little more than a matter of covering distance. Both campaigns ended in disaster for much the same reasons: the resilience of the Russians was underestimated, and so were the difficulties of supply. For Napoleon the main problem was shortage of fodder for his horses; for the Germans the shortage of fuel for their machines. For Napoleon the inadequacy of the roads; for the Germans the difference between the European and Russian railway-gauges. These were more determining factors even than the bitter cold of winter, for given a workable system of supply, both armies might have avoided their terrible fates.

It is necessary to anticipate events slightly in order to explain Napoleon's problem. On leaving Dresden he admitted that he was embarking upon 'the greatest and most difficult enterprise that I have ever attempted'. Hitherto he had never waged a campaign with more than 200,000 troops, or started with an army larger than his opponent's. Now he was about to lead more than twice that number into a country which extended halfway round the world, containing minimum food supplies, which would be reduced to almost nothing by the Russian scorched-earth policy, and in a climate which would start excessively hot and end excessively cold. Therefore he must make it a quick campaign, and organize an elaborate system of supply. He must take everything with him for at least two months. In this he failed. Some historians have concluded that before the coming of the railways and the electric telegraph to transmit his orders, he could not possibly have succeeded. The army was too big for the resources of the country to sustain it, or for the wretched roads to supply it. It was too extravagantly equipped, except for the remoter transport services on which it depended. It was accompanied by another army of bakers, tailors, masons, shoe-makers, gunsmiths, camp-followers and historians. Senior officers thought it essential to take with them the luxuries to which they were accustomed at home, including carpets for their tents, plate for their tables and servants for their comfort, and thought nothing of accommodating their staffs in carriages or cabriolets, and their personal baggage in half a dozen waggons. The troops, on a diminishing scale, imitated their commanders. Thus a division would draw behind it a supply-train, including hundreds of cattle on the hoof, which far exceeded in road space the distance occupied by the troops themselves, blocking the progress of the main food and ammunition convoys which followed them. Although there were adequate supplies in the nine vast depots from Warsaw to Königsberg (Danzig alone held rations for fifty days for 400,000 men), they could not reach the front. The distances and delays became so great that a convoy, even if it could push its way through, would consume *en route* a third of the supplies it carried. The draught-oxen seized in Poland and Prussia could eventually be eaten, but the horses, of which there were 200,000 in the supply-columns alone, must at all costs be saved. They were the biggest consumers of all. Each needed nine kilos of fodder a day. They could not live off the grass. To sustain them on their arduous trek, they must be fed the oats which they were dragging forward for their grander cousins, the cavalry and artillery horses (which numbered over

100,000). Many were sent to graze off unripe rye, which caused their deaths in thousands.

Furthermore, the waggons were quite unsuited to the Russian tracks. They stuck in sand or mud. Their axles broke in the pot-holes and ditches. No replacement horses or carts were to be found, as on previous campaigns. Vast quantities of stores were dumped by the roadside. Napoleon had organized two hundred river-boats, but they could not be used, because the rivers flowed in the wrong direction, except for the Dvina, and its seaport, Riga, was never captured. The mills for grinding corn, and ovens to bake bread, could not keep up with the troops. The twenty-day ration with which each battalion set off was exhausted long before the estimated time. Slaughter of the cattle sustained them for a little longer. Then their only recourse was pillage, and there was little to pillage. The Grand Army began to starve soon after the campaign started. The sick could rely on little medical help, for the ambulance services were also inadequate or left too far in the rear. Dysentery, diptheria and typhus spread: 60,000 men died or fell seriously ill before scarcely a shot had been fired.

Napoleon left his options open. Although he hoped for a quick campaign, he realized that it might have to be divided into two seasons, an advance as far as Smolensk in 1812, its continuation to Moscow, and possibly St Petersburg, in the spring of 1813. Sometimes he declared this to be his intention. For example, to the Comte de Flahault he confided on 13 June, 'This is not going to be a matter of a single campaign. I shall pursue the Russians as far as the Dvina and Dnieper' – the Orsha gap. 'I shall form a sort of bridgehead between those two rivers, and behind them I shall establish 120,000 French troops.' Then he hesitated. He could not be so long absent from Paris. His momentum, and his own vitality, would not allow him to halt. More than once, at Vitebsk, and again at Smolensk, he considered pausing to consolidate his gains. But always pressure urged him onwards, the pressure of success, of terminating the beginning, of proving his infallibility.

The opposing forces were deployed, when the campaign opened, as indicated in the sketch map of the Vistula to the Dvina. It will be seen that the Grand Army was more concen-

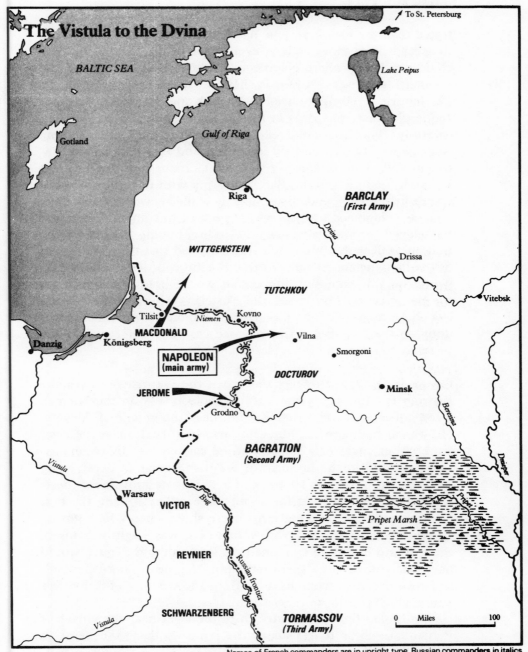

The Vistula to the Dvina

BALTIC SEA

Gotland

Gulf of Riga

To St. Petersburg

Lake Peipus

Riga

BARCLAY
(First Army)

Dvina

Drissa

Vitebsk

WITTGENSTEIN

TUTCHKOV

Tilsit

Niemen

Kovno

Vilna

Smorgoni

MACDONALD

Danzig

Königsberg

NAPOLEON
(main army)

DOCTUROV

Minsk

JEROME

Grodno

Beresina

Dnieper

Vistula

BAGRATION
(Second Army)

Warsaw

Bug

VICTOR

Pripet Marsh

Pripet

REYNIER

Russian frontier

SCHWARZENBERG

Vistula

TORMASSOV
(Third Army)

0   Miles   100

Names of French commanders are in upright type, Russian commanders in italics trated than the Russians, who had fewer troops but were obliged to spread them more widely, even south of the Pripet, for they could not know where Napoleon would turn after crossing the Niemen: south-east towards Minsk, north-east towards St Petersburg, or straight ahead to Vitebsk and Smolensk. Schwarzenberg's Austrian Corps in the far south must also be watched carefully. The Russian screen was therefore very thin, leaving large gaps between their three armies, and they had no alternative initially than to identify Napoleon's main thrust and retreat before it, hoping to unite Barclay's army with Bagration's somewhere in the rear, and then check it while they mobilized their reserves. Napoleon's object was to prevent this union. Therefore he delayed Jerome's advance on Grodno, hoping to keep Bagration on or near the Bug. Each side expected that the manoeuvres of the flanking formations, in the directions of Riga and Minsk, would be side-shows. Wittgenstein would hold Macdonald on the Baltic coast, Tormassov the Austrians wherever the Austrians chose to go. The main danger to Napoleon was Chichagov's army on the Danube, but he guessed correctly that it would not be ready to intervene for at least six weeks.

On 22 June 1812 (the very day when the Germans crossed the Russian frontier 129 years later) Napoleon was on the Niemen a few miles upstream from Kovno, near the village of Aleyota. He was in high spirits. The army was held back from the river bank under cover of a forest, and he carried out his reconnaissance dressed in the uniform of a Polish hussar to deceive any Cossack patrol on the far bank. There was no movement there. He rode down the river for about three miles, seeking the best crossing-point. At one place his horse shied when a hare got up between its hooves and threw him. He was slightly bruised. Some found in this an evil omen. 'A Roman', said Ségur, 'would have abandoned the expedition,' but Napoleon laughed it off, and resumed his reconnaissance from the window of a doctor's house which overlooked the stream.

He decided finally on a stretch of the river near the village of Poniemen, where it was about the same width as the Seine in Paris. He ordered three pontoon bridges to be thrown across, and while these were being prepared, he sent over a company of sappers in dinghies. They found the far bank deserted, but penetrating a little way into the forest beyond it they were confronted by a Cossack officer who demanded to know what they were doing there. They replied, according to Count Roman Soltyk, a Pole who was with them, 'To make war on you. To take Vilna. To free Poland!' This was, in effect, Napoleon's only declaration of war. He considered that the diplomatic exchanges of the previous year had made any other unnecessary.

The sappers were followed by 300 riflemen to protect the bridging site, and between 10 pm and 1 am on 24 June the pontoons were launched. Immediately the first troops, Morand's division, part of Davout's corps, began marching over, breaking their step to avoid swinging the bridges to the point of collapse. At dawn on the 24th Napoleon watched as three long columns wound out of the forest. As he hummed *Malbrouk s'en va-t-en guerre*, they greeted him with shouts of enthusiasm. The crossing continued for three days: 130,000 infantry and cavalry at this single point. At the same time Macdonald went over the Niemen at Tilsit, eighty miles downstream, and Jerome approached Grodno, the same distance south, but he did not cross the river till the 30th. Napoleon himself rode over on the morning of the 24th, and turned north to enter the town of Kovno, where he established his headquarters in a convent for the next three days.

So far all had gone well. Napoleon had achieved surprise. But as the Grand Army pressed on towards Vilna, seventy miles away, the logistic difficulties began to show. It seems incredible, as each soldier carried four days' rations in his knapsack, that long before they reached Vilna, against no opposition, men were falling out through exhaustion and hunger, and the horses were dying in hundreds by the road. The rations were all consumed, through indiscipline, on the first day. The storms which drenched them at the start were so explosive that they mistook the thunder for cannon-fire. The muddy tracks sucked at their boots and became almost impassable for carts. The rustic bridges collapsed under the weight of guns and heavy waggons. The first carriages were abandoned. Diarrhoea weakened the greener troops. The wells were found polluted by dead horses thrown into them by the Russians. Meat was unobtainable, as the cattle were left far behind. The few villages could scarcely provide sustenance for a platoon, as this was before the harvest. There was no shelter during the short nights, because the few peasant huts were verminous and leaked the water that dripped upon them from the trees. Following the rain came almost tropical heat. It dried the tracks, but the dust was stifling and so thick that drummers had to be stationed at the head of each short column to maintain direction. There were early desertions among the allied troops, and others died by suicide. Mortier, following the advance guard, summed up the conditions in a letter home:

> From the Niemen to Vilna, I have seen nothing but ruined houses and abandoned carts and equipment. 10,000 horses have been killed already by the cold rains and eating unripe rye which they are not accustomed to. The smell of the dead horses on the road is perfectly horrible. But that is not so bad as the shortness of rations. Several of my Young Guard have already starved to death.

Vilna provided a little opportunity for recuperation. The town was captured on 28 June almost unopposed. The Russians in abandoning it had destroyed the store and the bridge over the Vilya. Napoleon ordered the Polish cavalry to swim the river, but most of the horses were caught by the current in midstream, and as the riders were swept away, they turned to him with a dying shout of 'Vive l'Empereur', in recognition that he had led them to the liberation of the capital of Lithuania, which until its annexation by the Russians in 1795 had shared its sovereignty with Poland. The Grand Army was at first welcomed with the same elation as had been shown to Alexander two weeks earlier. The Comtesse de Choiseul-Gouffier, a Pole but maid-of-honour to the Tsarina, who was in the town at the time, wrote later: 'I can find no words to describe my emotion when I saw some Polish troops. They were galloping at full speed, sabres drawn yet laughing, waving their lance-pennants, which were in the national colours. I was wearing them myself for the first time. I stood at an open window, and they saluted me as they passed. I was going to become Polish again! Tears of joy and enthusiasm streamed down my face. That was a delicious moment, but it was not to last long.' The French began to loot.

All the remaining stores were exhausted within the first twenty-four hours. The houses were filled with troops. Every horse was commandeered (one woman attempted to save hers by hiding them in her first-floor drawing-room), but there was nothing to feed to them, as they would not eat the oats impregnated with the smoke of the burning magazines. Caulaincourt wrote that there were very few inhabitants left, 'only a few Jews and people of the lowest class', but this is not confirmed by other accounts. Some were hostile, some indifferent, but the majority hoped that Napoleon would proclaim the reincorporation of Lithuania within a free Poland. After all, his proclamation to his troops on 22 June had stated, 'Soldiers, the second Polish war has begun.' A deputation of leading Vilna citizens waited on him to tell him that the Poles in Warsaw had declared their independence of Russia and Poland's kingdom re-established, as he (they thought) had promised, but Napoleon was evasive, balancing the advantage of harnessing Polish nationalism to his cause against the fear and reproaches it would cause in Austria. He told them that he would think it over. The Vilna people were not too discouraged. They celebrated the Warsaw declaration by a Mass in the Cathedral, where the entire congregation was dressed in Polish colours, and staged a gala ball. The contrasts were pathetic. As they were fawning upon Napoleon in their palace, his newly appointed sub-prefect of Newtroki (outside Vilna) arrived almost naked to take up his post, stripped by French Grenadiers.

Vilna had been Alexander's headquarters when Napoleon crossed the Niemen. He had heard the news as he was attending a ball given by one of his closest advisers, General Bennigsen, whose estate was at Zakret outside the town, and returned immediately to Vilna, leaving the guests to continue dancing in happy ignorance of their danger. His first reaction was to send to Napoleon an emissary, his Minister of Police, Balashov, not to offer peace, but to demand an explanation why Napoleon was invading his country without even a declaration of war. Balashov reached the French outposts, then at Rossienti, midway between the Niemen and Vilna. He was escorted to Murat, then to

Davout, who ordered him, without consulting Napoleon, to march with the army to Vilna. There, on 30 June, he was at last admitted to Napoleon's presence, who received him in the very same room where he had been given his instructions by the Tsar a week before. He brought with him a letter from Alexander:

Monsieur mon frère, I heard yesterday that in spite of the loyalty with which I have kept faith with Your Majesty, your troops have invaded Russia. If Your Majesty is not determined to spill the blood of our people in an unnecessary war and will withdraw, I will regard this event as something that has not happened and we can come to terms. If not, I shall be obliged to resist an attack which I have done nothing to provoke. It rests with Your Majesty to prevent the calamity of another war.

The audience was brisk and final. Balashov said that he had nothing to add to the Tsar's letter. Napoleon must withdraw. The Emperor replied that Alexander must be joking. 'Does he imagine that I have come as far as Vilna to trade treaties? I have come to finish it off, once and for all.' The sword had been drawn: it could not be sheathed. 'The Russians will be thrust back into their snows and ice so that for a quarter of a century they will not be able to interfere with civilized Europe. Now that the Tsar sees that it is a serious matter, and that his army has already been cut in two, he is afraid and wants to come to terms. Tell him that I will sign the peace in Moscow.' His army was three times larger than Alexander's. He had already conquered an entire province without firing a shot. The Russians should be ashamed of surrendering Vilna. Balashov assured him that the Russians would fight 'a terrible war'. Napoleon: 'With all Europe behind me, how can you resist me?' Balashov: 'We shall do what we can, Sire.' Napoleon, scarcely attempting to justify himself, heaped insults upon the Russians. They were weak. Their generals were incompetent – only Bagration was any good. The Tsar was not fit to command. He was not a soldier, only an Emperor by inheritance. He had left the field of Austerlitz in tears. The Russians could expect no help from England. The British were already on their knees, as Russia would be within a month. Sweden and Turkey would soon join France. Then where would Russia be? He sent by Balashov a letter to Alexander, reminding him that at Tilsit the Tsar had promised to act 'as a second in your duel with England'. 'Your Majesty', he wrote, 'was the first to mobilize and to threaten my frontiers,' demanding the evacuation of Prussia. 'From that moment Your Majesty and I were at war.' So he had crossed the Niemen, 'profoundly convinced that I had done all I could to spare this fresh misfortune, whilst satisfying my own reputation, the honour of my people, and the sanctity of treaties'. It is one of the most cynical documents in the history of war.

Alexander had surrendered Lithuania because he was not yet organized to fight a major battle. His two main armies were split. The climax might come at Vitebsk, possibly at Smolensk, where they could unite. So the retreat must continue. He was not deliberately drawing Napoleon into the vastness of Russia in the hope that distance would destroy him. He could not give up his western provinces without arousing strong protests that his strategy was cowardly. He determined to stand as far west as possible, and he settled on the river-line of the Dvina, based upon his fortress at Drissa, and held it with 120,000 troops. But what fortress can resist a mobile strategy? This was no longer the Middle Ages. It need not be invested; it could be bypassed, and its garrison cut off. Drissa was the conception of the Tsar's Prussian adviser, Colonel Pfuel. Its defences had been under construction for six months by 2,000 men, and were complete. It was strong as an island is strong, but, unlike an island, was surrounded by unlimited land. When Bennigsen came to inspect it, he found it a folly. The fortifications were a trap. The river Drissa, a tributary of the Dvina, was behind the fortress. Was that security? Or an obstacle to retreat? He reported that 'I was surprised to find that it was the most disadvantageous position I have ever seen.' Even if it were strategically necessary to hold it, 'the works are badly sited and worse executed', not mutually supportive and allowing an enemy to approach through woods and folds in the ground. There were fords on both flanks. The French could cross behind it or ignore it completely. Clausewitz, who was then serving with the Russian army, agreed. Pfuel was only a theorist; he knew nothing of warfare except from books, and he knew nothing of Russia – he could not even speak the language.

The decision to abandon Drissa, and the consequent humiliation of Pfuel, exposed the lack of a Russian strategy and the incongruity of the Tsar's assumption of supreme command. Alexander was not an able soldier. In theory the leader of a great nation should command in war as well as in peace, as Alexander the Great had done, the Roman Emperors, Frederick the Great, Peter the Great and Napoleon himself. But the risk of entrusting strategy to a man who was untrained for it and not an instinctive field marshal was twofold – that he might make irremediable mistakes, and that his prestige as head of state would be weakened, if not destroyed, by reverses in the field. He could dismiss his generals, but his would be the ultimate responsibility for failure. Besides, there was the risk that if he remained at the front he might be surrounded and captured. In an autocratic state that could mean the end of the campaign. The army needed a less exalted leader. The Tsar's duty was to lead the nation, remote from its battlefields. His role lay in St Petersburg and Moscow, where he would be surrounded by his Court, whose presence at a military headquarters would only induce sycophancy and prevent frank discussion. A council-of-war would assume the character of a levée.

But how could this idea be communicated to a Tsar who was young, eager to lead his army, intensely patriotic, and deeply conscious of his responsibility and inheritance? The awkward task was given to Balashov. Alexander saw the sense in his argument, wrapped as it was in courtly language, and agreed to go. He left the army for Moscow on 14 July, handing over the command to Barclay at an interview in a stable, where Barclay was eating a meagre supper. Embracing him, he said, 'General, goodbye. I entrust my army to you. Do not forget that it is the only one I have. Always bear that in mind.' It was a solemn moment, and his words left Barclay with the conviction that he need not feel ashamed of acting cautiously. His main task was to keep the army intact, even if it meant constant retreat.

CHAPTER THREE

SMOLENSK

At Vilna Napoleon thought his army strategically well placed. He had already advanced deep enough, and with time enough, to defeat Barclay and Bagration separately, and then push between their shattered armies to the interior of Russia, where he would dictate the peace. He would throw against Barclay the mass of the Grand Army, and against Bagration Davout's corps together with Jerome's and Poniatowski's Poles. Then he would be in a position to advance on either St Petersburg or Moscow, intending Moscow but leaving his opponents in doubt which it was to be, so further dividing their remaining forces. His initiative was absolute, his success until this moment unbroken. He had created consternation and replenished fear.

It did not work out as he had planned. Bagration escaped. Barclay abandoned Drissa. They united at Smolensk. There was no major battle which could destroy either of them separately.

As soon as he entered Vilna, Napoleon sent Oudinot and Ney in pursuit of Barclay, and Davout in the direction of Minsk to cut off Bagration, who was retreating from Jerome. Both French Generals were dilatory, but it was on Jerome, his younger brother, that Napoleon's reproaches fell most heavily – and unfairly, because Davout's interception would only have succeeded if Bagration had not been pressed too hard in his retreat from the Niemen. As a mark of his displeasure ('you are compromising the whole success of the campaign on the right flank. It is impossible to carry on war in this fashion'), Napoleon placed his brother under Davout's direct command, and Jerome took the humiliation so badly that he resigned his mission and returned to Kassel, the capital of his kingdom of Westphalia. Davout entered Minsk on the heels of Bagration and did not catch up with him till Bobruisk. The manoeuvre (see sketch-map) had the advantage of preventing Bagration from moving north to join Barclay at Drissa or Vitebsk, but it did not succeed in trapping him.

Meanwhile, at Vilna, Napoleon pretended that all was going according to plan. Receiving the Polish deputies at dinner (according to Baron Jomini, the historian and Governor of Vilna, who was present), he opened the conversation by asking them how far it was to Moscow, a question to which he well knew the answer because he had studied maps all day. '250 leagues,' they replied, inaccurately, because it was less. Napoleon said that he would be there within six weeks. 'Oh, certainly. Your Majesty could easily be in Moscow in less time than that.' Napoleon replied, laughing, 'I'd much prefer to get there in two years' time. It is easy for you political gentlemen to cover distances like that. If General Barclay thinks that I want to run after him all the way to the Volga, he is much mistaken. We shall follow him as far as Smolensk, where a good battle will enable us to go into cantonments. I shall return with my headquarters to Vilna to spend the winter. I shall send for an opera company and actors from Paris. Then next May we shall finish the job, if we do not make peace during the winter.' This plan, of course, was a false trail intended for Barclay's ears, but it was one which Napoleon began to entertain with increasing seriousness.

He remained at Vilna too long (28 June to 16 July), repeating the mistake he had attributed to Jerome, for, though his corps were now spread over a wide distance beyond it, he was not present in person to direct and hasten their movements. He hoped that the Russians would be demoralized by their retreat, but it was his own army that suffered more. The march from Vilna to Vitebsk was conducted in the heat of mid-summer, broken at night by violent hail-storms. Marching through seemingly endless pine-forests, their eyes and mouths clogged with dust, or wading through marshes up to their waists, the troops' discipline soon began to crack. There were fierce altercations between different units and different arms. The commander of a Bavarian division reported to his King, 'There is such a widespread spirit of depression, discouragement, discontent,

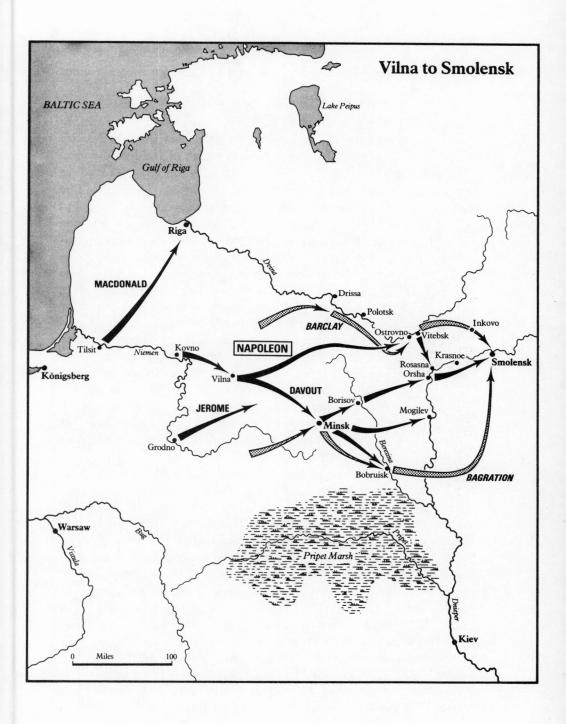

disobedience and insubordination that one cannot forecast what will happen.'

By mid-July the horses were in a pitiful state, sweating so heavily that within a few days they were covered in pus-running sores, or in such pain from the night cold that they frantically broke their halters. They were always short of fodder. General Belliard, Chief-of-Staff to Murat's cavalry corps, reported to Napoleon direct: 'Your Majesty must be told the truth. The cavalry is rapidly disappearing. The marches are too long and exhausting, and when a charge is ordered, you can see that the brave fellows are forced to stay behind because their horses cannot be put to the gallop.' For the supply columns conditions were even worse. The drivers soon put their own salvation before the army's desperate need of the stores they carried, and were relieved when the horses died or the carts broke and could be abandoned. At least 8,000 horses perished between Vilna and Vitebsk. The cattle, which had never in their lives been required to walk further than from field to farmyard, and farmyard ultimately to market, were incapable of these forced marches. 'There you have the secret and cause of our early disasters,' wrote Caulaincourt, who as Master of the Horse had an overall responsibility. The hardships of the summer were as destructive of the army as the rigours of the winter, but even in retrospect Napoleon refused to admit it.

The Russians appeared not to be suffering to the same extent. The invaders found no dead horses by the roadside, no stragglers, no jettisoned stores, cannon, or sick men. In fact their commissariat was as inefficient as Napoleon's. They had main depots to retreat upon, but on the march they too were without food, water and fodder, and the instruction to 'leave nothing to the enemy' meant that their rearguard found the country already devastated. The peasants were as scared of their own army as they were of the French. They fled, and their hamlets were razed. If by chance they found a lonely French soldier searching for a few potatoes, their revenge was merciless.

Napoleon maintained that his armies were accustomed to marching on empty stomachs, and tried to raise his men's spirits by promising them, as he had at Vilna, rest and comforts at Vitebsk. When he received the news that Barclay had abandoned

Drissa on the same day (16 July) as he left Vilna, he was at first amazed and overjoyed. He said to Berthier, 'You see, the Russians don't know how to make war or peace. They are a degenerate nation. They give up their fortress without firing a shot. Come along! One more real effort on our part and the Tsar will repent of having taken the advice of my enemies.'

There were constant brushes with the Cossacks, but Barclay's main army had vanished. Then on 25 July Murat came up with its reaguard at Ostrovno, on the banks of the Dvina a few miles west of Vitebsk. For a short while Napoleon was convinced that Barclay had at last decided to make a stand, and he delayed a day to bring up more troops. It turned out to be nothing but a skirmish, which held up the French for a few hours, but it was the first engagement of the campaign, and gave Murat an opportunity to display his mettle and Eugène his calm. The rest of the Grand Army watched from the encircling hills, applauding the feats of their comrades as if in an amphitheatre. Barclay withdrew to the plateau which lay in front of Vitebsk, bounded by the river to its north. Was this, then, his chosen battlefield? Murat assured the Emperor that it was. Napoleon displayed his utmost energy ('beaming with pride', says Caulaincourt), and remained with his advance posts at dawn on 27 July. He saw the Russian army drawn up in battle order, some 80,000 strong, he estimated, and deployed his own. As was his custom, he rested his troops that day in expectation of a major battle on the morrow, engaging only a few units to improve his opening positions, and reconnoitring on horseback every corner of the ground. During the night the Russians silently retired to many miles beyond the town. A single soldier was found on the plateau, asleep under a bush. It later became known that Barclay had intended to fight, but had changed his mind on learning that Bagration was again retreating and could offer him no help. Indeed, it is difficult to understand why he ever conceived it to be possible, as Bagration was 150 miles south, blocked by Davout. Barclay was too greatly outnumbered to fight alone.

Napoleon entered Vitebsk at 8 am on 29 July, and rode beyond the town for some distance to discover which route the Russians had taken, but found no sign of their retreat except cart-tracks which indicated the general direction of Smolensk. He returned to Vitebsk and remained there for two weeks. The population of 20,000, apart from the poorest class, the sick and the wounded, had abandoned it. There was no information to be gained from any of them. 'We were like a vessel without a compass in the midst of a vast ocean,' wrote Caulaincourt with scant exaggeration. Napoleon declared the province to be part of Poland and ordered that the inhabitants should be treated as allies, not subjects. The town was unburnt and there were some supplies. Convoys, stragglers and a few reinforcements trickled in. The French wounded were placed in the hospitals alongside the Russian. Conditions in them were deplorable. There was a shortage of doctors, medical supplies and even of bandages, for which were substituted shirts torn from dead men's backs. Infection spread everywhere. Those who had lost a limb died first.

Napoleon set up his headquarters in the modest Governor's Palace, and ordered the square in front of it to be cleared of ramshackle buildings to give his troops more room to parade at six each morning. His mood alternated between anger at being cheated once again of a major battle and exhilaration that he had occupied unopposed the first city in Old Russia, but more often it was irritability. Berthier was 'snapped at all day long', and capable, devoted generals were dismissed like scullions from his presence. He issued orders that were impossible to execute, since they presumed supplies and materials that only existed far in the rear, and complained of every shortage without having the power to remedy it. For form's sake he ordered that any man caught looting was to be shot, but said nothing when the order was disobeyed, knowing that loot was an essential substitute for supply and that he had previously announced that the army would live as far as possible off the country.

His main preoccupation was with strategy. His flank armies caused him little concern, though they gave him little help. Macdonald had advanced to invest Riga, where he was reinforced by the army's siege-train, and Oudinot and St Cyr were manoeuvring against Wittgenstein further down the Dvina. In the south Bagration was retiring fast before Davout, and Schwarzenberg and Reynier were engaging Tormassov in a humdrum campaign which at this stage scarcely affected the plans of either main army.

The problem was in the centre, at Vitebsk itself, the tip of the spear which Napoleon had driven deep into Russia. Should he remain there for the entire winter and revitalize the army? Or should he continue his advance against an enemy which would shortly be united at Smolensk? Unrolling huge maps and placing on them his sword with an air of decision, he at first said that the campaign of 1812 was over: 'We won't repeat Charles XII's folly.' He would rest his men and horses, bring up supplies, send to Paris for a theatrical troupe, and await Alexander's offer of peace. This mood was not to last more than twenty-four hours. Inaction irritated him. It was undignified for a conqueror to pause. He could not delay eight months when twenty days would bring him to Moscow. Pacing up and down he threw questions at his staff to which he did not welcome any answers. When Berthier, Duroc and Caulaincourt advised him to stay, saying that Barclay was only luring them deeper into Russia, he rounded on them, accusing them of being soft: he had made them too rich and grand. To another general he said, 'You were born on a campaign, and you will die on one.' When Daru, his chief quartermaster, bravely remonstrated, 'Not only our troops, Sire, but we ourselves fail to understand the aim or necessity of this war,' and that the problem of supply could only worsen if they advanced, Napoleon's indignation at the impertinence finally decided him. He would pursue the Russians at least as far as Smolensk and fight a battle which would end the campaign. Gradually he wore down his staff's resistance. Murat agreed with him. To remain at Vitebsk was insupportable, to retreat unthinkable: so they must advance. The Grand Army set off on 11 August.

The Russians had by now widened the gap between them and their pursuers, and their reunion at Smolensk was in little doubt. They had won temporary safety by a manoeuvre which Bagration found disgraceful. As early as 8 July he had written to Arakcheyev, Alexander's former Minister of War, that he found himself in an impossible position: 'I don't know why we are ordered to withdraw. Nobody in the army or country will believe that we are not traitors.' They should retake Vilna, and when Vitebsk was lost, Vitebsk. 'Let us advance all along the line. There lies honour and glory.' His anger was directed mainly against Barclay, but he implied also the Tsar. The mistake had been in their initial dispositions, and in underestimating the size of the army with which Napoleon had crossed the Niemen. Now there was no agreed strategy. Liprandi, quartermaster to Docturov's Sixth Corps, wrote afterwards: 'Neither before Smolensk nor until Moscow itself did we have any defined plan of action. Everything happened according to circumstances.' The 'Scythian plan' to withdraw was a later invention to excuse it, conceived because it happened to fit in well with what subsequently occurred. If, as Tolstoy comments in *War and Peace*, the plan had been to decoy the French into the heart of the country, there was no point in seeking to unite the two Russian armies. They could have melted separately into the distance. Bagration's southern flank march had the incidental advantage of dividing the French and enabling him to draw reinforcements from the Ukraine. It also suited his temperament, loud as he was in his protests against it. He was on his own, protected by distance from coming under the direct command of Barclay, whom he despised, and was executing a withdrawal with a skill that could only earn him credit. If disaster ensued, he could claim that he had warned against it. But it was to Barclay, who 'had an almost uncanny instinct for avoiding a blunder' (Alan Palmer), that Alexander listened.

The convergence of Barclay and Bagration at Smolensk meant that Napoleon's own main army would be united in the same place, and he had about 185,000 men to bring against 125,000 Russians. They had time to prepare for him. They reached Smolensk – Barclay first, Bagration two days later – a fortnight before Napoleon left Vitebsk. The meeting of the two Generals was frosty with mutual reproach. Barclay told the Tsar that he had to flatter Bagration to gain his co-operation ('a manner I find most repugnant, and one totally contrary to my character and feelings'). Each accused the other of abandoning key cities without a fight. Barclay had lost Vilna and Vitebsk; Bagration, Minsk and Mogilev. What were they to do now? They could take the initiative by advancing from Smolensk to meet Napoleon in a pitched battle in the Orsha gap, or they could hold Smolensk like a fortress till winter. Barclay's indecision, and Bagration's smouldering resentment, led to the adoption, and failure, of each plan in turn. The whole army, in three branching columns, at first advanced cautiously into the country north of the Dnieper, leaving only one regiment in Smolensk and one division south of the river at Krasnoe. They failed to find the French, halted, and then pulled back towards the city, while Barclay's patrols continued to search for any hint of Napoleon's intentions. So poor were the intelligence services on both sides that they lost each other for several days. Smolensk might be another Drissa, a trap which Napoleon might close behind them by a lightning move. If he simply bypassed the town, the road to Moscow would be open to him. This seemed unlikely, as he desired a great battle as much as the Russians, now that they were united, and the choice was between resisting his attack within the medieval walls, or facing him in open country close to them. It depended upon the direction of his advance. If he took the normal route, along the Minsk–Smolensk–Moscow highway, he would remain north of the River Dnieper, where there were few prepared defences, and it would be an open battle. If he crossed the river and attacked the fortified city from the west and south, it would be a siege.

Napoleon decided, against all probability, to cross the river. He heard that on 8 August his advance cavalry under Sebastiani had clashed with the Cossacks at Inkovo, north-west of Smolensk, and although the French came off rather the worse from the encounter, he was delighted to have his suspicion confirmed that Barclay was heading in that direction, away from Smolensk. He would get behind him by transporting the great mass of his army across the Dnieper and sieze Smolensk by a rapid advance along the left (southern) bank. This great manoeuvre failed, because Barclay abandoned his western thrust just in time. That his nerve failed him is unquestionable, but his retreat was also due to Bagration's unreliability as a subordinate and his own fear of Napoleon's reputation for doing the unexpected. It was a moment of great crisis. Large forces on both sides were circling round each other, probing for information without success, and knowing that the first major confrontation of the campaign was impending.

Napoleon crossed the Dnieper on a fifteen-mile front between Orsha and Rosasna. There was a bridge at Orsha, unguarded, and at Rosasna the French engineers completed four pontoon bridges during the night of 13/14 August. By dawn next day, 175,000 troops were south of the river, so far undetected. Only Sebastiani's light cavalry division remained on the right bank. Murat immediately hurried east towards Smolensk, and at Krasnoe, thirty miles from the town, he encountered Neveroski's division of 8,000 men and 1,500 cavalry, which Barclay had wisely stationed there before he knew of Napoleon's manoeuvre. There was a sharp fight, Murat leading a series of charges against the Russian infantry, which formed squares behind the cavalry. A defile, and Murat's conviction that he could break through unaided, prevented the artillery and Ney's infantry from joining him, and Neveroski was able to retreat in good order to Smolensk, where he joined Raevski's corps. They were the only troops available to hold it. Barclay and Bagration were still hastening back from their aborted offensive. Napoleon, if he had displayed the same energy as after leaving Vitebsk, could have rushed the position. Instead, for the rest of that day, 14 August, he slowed the advance. It was said that he wished to review his troops on the 15th, his forty-third birthday, but this is improbable. When he heard one hundred cannon discharged to honour him, he protested against the waste of ammunition, and recovered his temper only when told that the artillery had used Russian powder captured at Krasnoe, together with seven cannon, the first trophies of the campaign. Next morning, 16 August, he rode forward to the outskirts of Smolensk itself and reconnoitred its defences.

It is an ancient city, one of the holiest in Russia, built on high bluffs each side of the Dnieper. The old city lay on the south bank, encircled by a seventeenth-century crenellated brick wall four miles long and on average thirty feet high and fifteen feet thick at its base. It was punctuated by thirty-three rectangular and polygonal turrets extruded from the wall-face, some in ruins, but others still strong enough to carry cannon. In one corner was a citadel called the King's Bastion, doubly ringed by fortifications. Outside the defences were a number of suburbs, of which the most important, the St Petersburg suburb, lay on the north bank, linked to the old city by a wooden bridge, which became the focus of the fighting, as it was the only route by

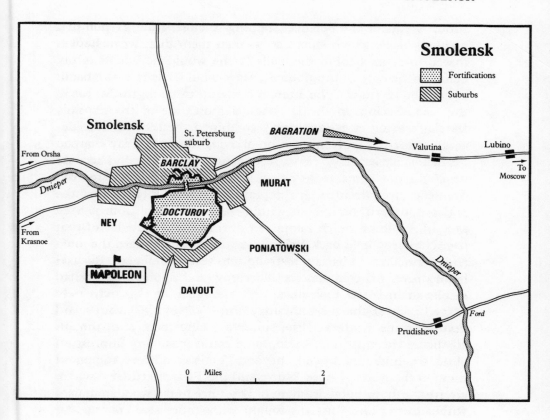

Smolensk

Fortifications

Suburbs

Smolensk

St. Petersburg suburb

BAGRATION

Valutina

Lubino

To Moscow

From Orsha

BARCLAY

Dnieper

MURAT

DOCTUROV

NEY

From Krasnoe

PONIATOWSKI

Dnieper

NAPOLEON

DAVOUT

Ford

Prudishevo

0   Miles   2

which Raevski's corps could be supplied and reinforced. As soon as the main Russian army arrived, it occupied the north bank, including the St Petersburg suburb, leaving the fortress to be defended by about 20,000 men and seventy guns. There was no room for more, and if Napoleon succeeded in capturing it and crossing the river he would confront Barclay and Bagration on the far side. He decided that he had no alternative but to attack it frontally, since if he attempted a crossing further east, where there were fords, he would leave the Russians astride his communications. A younger Napoleon would have taken the risk, and Barclay was well aware that he still might. The Russian's caution had a decisive effect on the battle.

Raevski at first bravely occupied in strength the southern

53

suburbs outside the defences, hoping to engage the French in a mauling battle which would so weaken them that, when he was forced to retire behind the walls (as he would be bound to do, being so heavily outnumbered), they would hesitate to assault them. On 16 August the French came up in strength, Murat in the lead. Seeing on the far bank a multitude of troops, now Barclay's army and Bagration's combined, he sent an aide-de-camp to alert Napoleon, who on arriving about midday clapped his hands, exclaiming, *'Enfin, je les tiens!,'* optimistically, because he could not come to grips with them till the battle for old Smolensk was decided. He deployed his four corps round the entire southern perimeter within range of the suburbs (see sketch). Nothing much happened during the remainder of that day. Napoleon held back, using his artillery to bombard the town and skirmishers in battalion strength to test its defences. Raevski handed over his command to Docturov, and rejoined Bagration.

The main battle took place on 17 August. It was extremely fierce. Each of the three infantry corps – Ney's, Davout's and Poniatowski's – attacked the suburbs facing them and, though all succeeded in gaining them, none could make any impression upon the high, thick walls beyond. Veteran officers compared them to the walls of Acre. Nor could the French artillery, which after a five-hour bombardment only set fire to the wooden houses within them. The Russians fought with impressive courage. 'A number of our first attacks', wrote Ségur, 'ended in failure about twenty paces from the Russian front. They would again and again suddenly turn to face us and throw us back by rifle fire. They had to be restrained by their officers from charging, and light wounds were ignored until they fell from exhaustion and loss of blood.' A Russian artillery officer allowed the French to approach within 200 yards and then let fly with case-shot. The sight was so horrible that it dismayed both sides. 'I had often seen soldiers fall,' wrote a Russian eye-witness, 'but never had I seen so many felled by a single salvo, weltering in their own blood and without arms or legs.... I felt completely forsaken, and I was suddenly overcome with such fear that I would willingly have hidden in a mousehole.'

The battle died down at dusk, with the French in possession of the southern suburbs, the Russians of the town. Smolensk was now one vast conflagration. Stendhal wrote to Félix Faure that it was 'a fine spectacle'. Napoleon, watching it, agreed. He exclaimed to Caulaincourt, 'An eruption of Vesuvius! Is that not a fine sight, my Master of Horse?' 'Horrible, Sire.' 'Bah! Remember, gentlemen, what one of the Roman Emperors said: "The corpse of an enemy always smells good."' The staff giggled nervously, but most of them were profoundly shocked.

It was not only his vulgarity that horrified these men of gentle birth, but the hint it gave that Napoleon would withdraw from a promise he had made to Caulaincourt earlier that day. It had gradually become clear to them that the Russians were about to surrender the town and retreat. Long columns of troops had been seen moving eastwards, and towards evening men in increasing numbers were dashing over the bridge from the fortress to join them, clearly not in panic but in organized groups. Napoleon said that, in that case, he would be satisfied with the capture of Smolensk. He would drive the Russians a little further back for his security, then hold his position, and establish his winter headquarters at Vitebsk. So, at least, he said to Caulaincourt. But to Murat, according to Ségur, he took the opposite line. Murat advised him not to attack the retreating Russians, but to remain in Smolensk. Napoleon replied that he wanted Moscow. The argument flared. Murat appealed to him again that he was courting disaster. Throwing himself on his knees before his Emperor, he declared, 'Moscow will destroy us!' Napoleon told him to hold his tongue, and Murat, as if inviting suicide, rode sullenly towards a French battery which was being shelled from the opposite bank. His staff begged him to move somewhere safer, as he would be 'killed without glory'. He paid no attention. They said that he was endangering the lives of all those with him. 'Well, leave me if you want.' They refused, and he tore himself away. That even Murat could advise caution at such a moment of triumph was a measure of the dilemma which faced Napoleon. It occupied his thoughts centrally for the next two weeks, as it had at Vitebsk.

It was true that the Russians were retreating again. Barclay had come increasingly to fear that Napoleon would re-cross the Dnieper by a ford at Prudishevo and take him in the rear. He ordered Bagration to move first, while the battle was still at its

height, and take up a position a long way down the Moscow
road, to provide, as it were, a long-stop. Barclay would follow a
few hours later. After dark Docturov would evacuate the old
town, using the two extra bridges which had been thrown over
beside the old one, and then burn all three when his last man
was across. A rearguard was to be left in the St Petersburg
suburb. The order aroused indignation among senior Russian
officers, a view shared by the Englishman, Sir Robert Wilson,
who had taken part in the battle. They thought it disgraceful
that so many brave men should have been sacrificed to no purpose, a holy city burnt, and Napoleon allowed, simply by the
fear he aroused in the General, to dictate Barclay's movements.
Instead of retreating, they said, he should have continued to hold
the town with 20,000 men, and with the bulk of the army descended on Napoleon's baggage-train from Orsha, slicing behind
the slicer. Bagration, of course, agreed. He wrote to Rostopchin,
Governor of Moscow, in these vituperative terms: 'That wretch,
that scoundrel, that vermin Barclay gave up a splendid position
for nothing. I swear to you that Napoleon was in the bag. He
never listens to me and does everything that is useful to the
enemy.' And to Arakcheyev: 'He may be all right in ministerial
matters [Barclay was still Minister of War], but as a General he's
not only poor but worthless.... He is most amiably leading a
guest to the capital.' Of course, by no conceivable fantasy could
Napoleon be said to be 'in the bag' at Smolensk, and two days
later he did exactly what Barclay had expected him to do. The
Russian army was saved by this 'worthless General's' prescience.

So during the night of 17/18 August the blazing ruins were
abandoned by its defenders, taking its holiest ikon with them,
the Black Virgin, and a French patrol entered before dawn.
When the troops had dowsed the fire, and had time to look
around them, the scenes they witnessed were appalling. The
town ditches, the banks of the river, the streets, were clogged
with dead. 'I walked through the mass of corpses,' wrote a
French officer, Duverger. 'The fire had carbonized them, and
shrunk them to the size of children.' He saw pigs rooting among
them, and French soldiers catching and roasting the pigs for
dinner. Another, quoted by Tarlé, wrote home: 'They lay there
in piles, charred, almost without human forms, among the smok-

ing ruins and flaming beams. The position of many of the corpses indicated the horrible torments that must have preceded death. I trembled with horror at the spectacle, which will always haunt my memory.' Cesare Loggie, an Italian officer with Eugène's corps, recalled: 'To the strains of military music, proudly and grimly we marched in among the ruins, where the unhappy Russian wounded wallowed in blood and mire. On the threshold of houses which had survived the fire stood groups of them imploring assistance. In the Cathedral, dead, dying, wounded, old men, young men, women and children, were lying in a heap. Entire families in rags, with horror on their faces, weeping, exhausted, famished, were huddled together round the altars. They all trembled at our approach.'

Almost the only one not to be sickened by the sight was Napoleon himself. He was accustomed to it. He walked through the streets and installed himself in the Governor's Palace, which was of brick and unburnt. He exclaimed, 'The scoundrels! Fancy abandoning such a position!' Then he dictated a letter to Maret, his Minister of Foreign Affairs:

I have this moment come in. The heat is intense, and there is a lot of dust, which we find rather trying. The enemy's whole army was here. It was under orders to fight, but dared not. We have captured Smolensk without the loss of a man. It is a very big town, with walls and pretty good fortifications. We killed three to four thousand of the enemy, wounded thrice as many, and found plenty of guns here. According to all accounts a number of their divisional generals were killed. The Russian army is marching towards Moscow in a very discouraged and discontented state.

The last sentence was true. The rest of the letter was a pitiless travesty of what had occurred. To report officially, even for the sake of opinion in Paris, that he 'had not lost a man' in the attack, when he had lost 8–9,000, and 100,000 more since he left the Niemen, is difficult to forgive. But the Russians, too, were not above self-deception. In St Petersburg a solemn *Te Deum* was sung to celebrate the 'victories' of Vitebsk and Smolensk. 'They lie to God as well as to men,' was Napoleon's comment.

On 18 August there were two further moves. The bridges were hastily restored, and before they were ready – the river was found to be fordable at a depth of four feet in places – detachments were sent across to the St Petersburg suburb, but were repelled by the Russian rearguard. Napoleon disregarded this minor reverse, for he had a more ambitious scheme in mind. His scouts had now found the Prudishevo ford, three miles east of Smolensk, and he ordered Junot to seize it, cross the river and intercept Barclay's retreat by forming a massive road-block at Lubino. Ney would advance along the north bank, and the Russians, or half of them (for Bagration was well clear by now), would be trapped. On 19 August Ney was at Valutina, Junot on the north bank of the river just beyond him, and Barclay, who had missed his way in the darkness with his whole army, between them. Ney rode over to Junot. 'Now finish the business. Glory and a Marshal's baton await you.' Although Ney attacked with vigour, Junot did not move, explaining alternately that his Württemberg cavalry refused to charge, and that his orders from Napoleon were to cross the river and wait. Napoleon's reprimand was unsparing: 'Junot has let them escape. He is losing the campaign for me,' just as he had said of Junot's predecessor in command of the Corps, Napoleon's brother Jerome. Murat was even more explosive. He told him, 'You are unworthy to be the last dragoon in Napoleon's army.' Junot had been Napoleon's sergeant-secretary at Toulon in 1793. He had been with him in Egypt and at Austerlitz, had fought in Spain, and was created Duc d'Abrantes for his exploits there. He fought at Borodino. But he never received his baton. He never recovered from his disgrace at Smolensk. His mind became deranged, and he threw himself to his death from a window in July 1813.

Very different was the fate and legend of General Gudin, mortally wounded at Valutina. He was brought, dying, to Napoleon in Smolensk, both legs lacerated, and the whole army mourned him when he was buried in the Citadel. Ségur said of him, 'He was just, gentle, able and honourable – a rare combination at a time when too often men of good character lacked ability, and men of ability lacked morals.' He was the first general in the Grand Army to lose his life in this campaign.

Barclay escaped the trap, and Murat took his cavalry to trail him on the Moscow road. The remaining troops rested for six days in Smolensk, and Napoleon debated once again whether to remain there or continue eastwards. At St Helena he said that to have left Smolensk in late August was the biggest strategic mistake of his life. At the time, the arguments for doing so seemed imperative. The Russian army was so far undefeated. Its main forces had not even been seriously engaged. It would grow more confident as it retired on its bases, and a winter's pause would give the Tsar time to recruit and train many thousands of men. He would bring his regular armies from Finland and the Danube. Moscow was only another 270 miles ahead, and prisoners told him that there was already panic there. The magnetic attraction of the city for him grew stronger as he came nearer. Once there, he could lodge his troops in greater comfort than in burnt and stinking Smolensk, and control the highways that radiated from it. Europe would be amazed at the daring and success of his enterprise, whereas if he remained in Smolensk his detractors would sneer that he had over-reached himself without being able to grasp the prize. Austria and Prussia might defect, seeing the prolongation of the campaign from one year to two as a sign of his failing powers. Then there was the old argument that he could not stay away from Paris so long. Besides, Alexander would certainly not offer terms to a conqueror who had halted two-thirds of the way, but he might be induced to parley after defeat in a big battle and the loss of his holy capital, Moscow. While he was still in Smolensk, he was confirmed in his opinion of Alexander's stubbornness by an interview he had there with a Russian officer, Count Orloff, who had come to him under a flag of truce to enquire after General Tutchkov, who had been captured, badly wounded, at Valutina. Napoleon asked him if the Russians would fight at least one battle, for their honour. 'Thereafter it would be easy to make peace, as between two champions reconciled after a duel.' The war, he said, was only a matter of politics. Orloff could return to his lines if he promised to convey this message direct to the Tsar. Orloff replied that he would do so, but he did not think peace was possible as long as the French remained on Russian soil.

The arguments for advancing now seemed to Napoleon so strong that he grew deaf to the objections raised by Murat,

Caulaincourt and all the other leading men except Davout. They begged him to consider the sorry state of his army, now reduced to 160,000 men, which would be further reduced by the garrisons he would have to leave behind him on the road. His troops were exhausted, his horses eating thatch. Increasing distances would make supply even more difficult than it had been hitherto. They would find nothing but devastation ahead. They were already deep in hostile territory, and the Russians had been aroused at Smolensk to heroic resistance which would only increase as the campaign neared Moscow. If they did turn to fight and Napoleon lost the battle, he would be in a desperate plight. If he won and entered Moscow, he would be incarcerated there by the winter for six months. He would be unable to move against St Petersburg, the political capital, until the spring and, in the interval, his pencil-thin supply-line would be cut. Far better to make Smolensk and Vitebsk his winter quarters, nearer his depots, nearer Paris, and so situated that he would leave the Russians guessing which was his 1813 objective. St Cyr's victory over Wittgenstein near Polotsk on the Dvina, of which they now heard, guarded his left flank, and even Schwarzenberg had had a minor success against Tormassov in the south-west. Napoleon still had time this year to capture Riga and Kiev, and with strong-points there, and others at Polotsk, Vitebsk and Smolensk, he could form a defensive screen behind which he could raise a new army from a liberated Poland.

Napoleon knew that the control of Europe lay wherever he happened to be himself. If he were victorious in the centre, everything else would fall into line. It scarcely mattered what happened at Riga or Brest-Litovsk, even in Vienna or Berlin, provided that the progress of the main army, with himself at its head, was unchecked. He was accustomed to master events. There is a momentum in great affairs as in small, he reminded Caulaincourt, which cannot be arrested. Excited by the false news that Barclay intended to stand at Dorogobouje, fifty miles away, he hastened to the front in a single day, taking his Guard with him, and though it came to nothing, it was this incident that made up his mind. The machine of war slipped inexorably into gear again. He ordered up Victor from the Niemen to garrison Smolensk and take command of the detachments at Minsk,

Mogilev and Vitebsk. Schwarzenberg was to capture Kiev, Macdonald Riga, and then advance on St Petersburg. St Cyr was to
move up the Dvina, Augereau to the Niemen. The Rhine and
Elbe garrisons were to be strengthened. Napoleon, now roused
to frenzied activity, was securing for himself a firm base to safe-
guard his supplies, and (did the thought strike him then?) in case
he had to retreat from Moscow. Meanwhile the main army would
advance. On 25 August they left Smolensk, eastwards.

There was also uncertainty in the Russian high command.
Barclay had saved the army, but only by retreating 400 miles in
seven weeks, which affronted its pride. Alexander had aroused
the spirits of the people by his bearing in Moscow. Both army
and people could be satisfied only by a major battle, and by
replacing Barclay by a commander who inspired confidence and
would fight. He chose Kutuzov.

Prince Michael Kutuzov was not the inevitable choice. Bennigsen or Bagration might have been preferable. Kutuzov was
sixty-seven, so corpulent that he could ride only with difficulty,
lethargic, a *bon viveur* given to drink and amorousness, but 'polished, courteous, shrewd as a Greek, naturally intelligent', as Sir
Robert Wilson described him. He had made his name fighting
the Turks, lost one eye in battle when he was twenty-nine, and
though he had been defeated at Austerlitz, he was the grand old
man of the Russian army, popular, brave, calm, professional and
cunning. His aide-de-camp, General Mayevsky, wrote of him:
'He was a Mozart or a Rossini who enchanted the ear with his
conversational grace. Nobody was more adept at playing on the
emotions, and nobody was subtler in the art of cajoling and
seducing.' He was cautious and he was lazy, sly more than in-
genious, jealous of subordinates, reluctant to read or sign a
paper, and difficult to advise or stimulate. Napoleon called him
'the Dowager'. Kutuzov had himself said, 'No general has any
enterprise after his forty-fifth year.' His object was to defeat
Napoleon with the minimum loss by playing a waiting game, a
strategy and attitude not so very different from Barclay's, but he
was at least a Russian, as Barclay was not, a Tartar, and by
default a hero. Kutuzov emerges well from Tolstoy's portrait of
him in *War and Peace*, because he represented 'the spontaneous
movement of the Russian people', a patriot, an elderly champion.

Alexander, who disliked him personally and had never forgiven him for Austerlitz, but was persuaded by his military council that nobody else would do, appointed him Commander-in-Chief on 20 August. Barclay was retained in command of the First Army and, oddly, as Minister of War. Bagration was to continue to command the Second Army. A Third Army (ignoring for the moment Tormassov's) was being raised in Moscow. So Kutuzov was given the role which today would be described as Army-Group Commander, and Alexander reluctantly added to it the title of Prince. It is said that the Tsar muttered to an intimate, 'Le public a voulu sa nomination. Je l'ai nommé. Quant à moi, je m'en lave les mains.'

Kutuzov joined the army as its commander at Tsarevo, between Viasma and Gzatsk, on 29 August. He travelled from St Petersburg in a droshky, still preserved in the museum at Borodino, which well illustrates his bulk, for there was room inside it only for one person, himself, and he needed to place one huge foot each side of a floor-partition. Barclay, though humiliated, received him well, since Kutuzov, far from reproaching him, implicitly agreed with all he had done. The French, however inadvertently, had been outwitted and weakened by this war of small engagements, and now the scorched earth and climate would take increasing toll. Clausewitz, who was still at Alexander's headquarters, wrote: 'Kutuzov, it is certain, would not have given battle at Borodino, where he obviously did not expect to win. But the voice of the Court, the army and all Russia forced his hand.' He was bound to fight.

CHAPTER FOUR
BORODINO

It is about 200 miles from Smolensk to Borodino. The route lies across the upland plateau formed by the headwaters of three major rivers, the Dvina, Dnieper and Volga, and two minor ones, the Moskva and Oka (see pp xii and xiii). The country, though occasionally split by ravines and often by forests, was gently rolling and quite richly cultivated. There were many villages and some large estates. The road, which Catherine the Great had constructed as her main strategic artery to the west, was a broad, sandy track reserved by Napoleon for his wheeled transports, artillery, ambulances and headquarters. The infantry marched across the open country on each side, with the cavalry on the outer flanks, Murat in the lead, Ney's corps on the left and Davout's on the right, and Eugène's 'Army of Italy' and Poniatowski's Polish Corps outside them on the left and right respectively. The whole army formed a frontage of about four miles, but not as neatly as this verbal picture might suggest, for the woods and ditches split and delayed them irregularly, and the hardship of the march caused a lengthening trail of stragglers.

Though there was little opposition from the Cossacks, other difficulties intensified. Marching up to thirty miles a day, they were stifled by dust or drenched by rain. In dry weather the heat was extreme. Against the wind-driven sand they shielded their faces by strips of cloth with holes cut in them for the eyes, as if in a desert, and improvised dark glasses with bits of windowpane to lessen the glare. Some covered their heads with foliage. Men were seen quenching their thirst with horse-urine, for water was unobtainable or polluted. The villages were in ruins. There was a severe shortage of food, and no time, given the urgency of the advance, to scour the country far from the road, so that those nearest to it, being more tightly concentrated, suffered most. The horses continued to die in thousands. In case the Cossacks became more active, they were kept saddled for sixteen hours a day, and as usual they were starving. The lush grass which then, as now, spreads across the plain was no substitute for hay and oats when the horses were being worked so hard. In any case, a cavalry horse will take about three hours to eat enough grass to sustain itself for a day, a heavier artillery or transport horse longer, and even if there had been time to let them graze, the fields within reach of the road would soon have been stripped by a single regiment. 'Being unable to sustain themselves on their patriotism,' said the sardonic General Nansouty, commanding the 1st Cavalry Corps, to Murat, 'they fall down by the roadside and expire.' A division which crossed the Niemen with 7,500 horses had less than 1,000 left at Borodino.

In 1941, nearly 130 years later, the hostility of the Russian climate, people and terrain imposed on the German troops hardships equal, and in many ways identical, to those endured by Napoleon's. They were advancing towards Moscow over the same wide plain, most of them marching twenty-five miles a day, 'on deep sandy tracks and with the sobering sight of the many foundering horses and the frequent jettisoning of vehicle loads', an infantryman wrote.* For months on end they had no change of clothes. In the villages they found no shelter, for if a cottage was unburnt, it was verminous. 'With the lack of transport all, even the sick, had to march and there could be no question of leaving anyone behind as the area was notorious for banditry. One day followed another, and the great chain of men moved forward in the slashing rain, obedient and silent, with nothing to be heard but the snorting of horses and the creak of the waggons and the everlasting roar of the wind in the firs on either side of the track.' This was in September 1941, the month of Borodino, 1812.

Napoleon did not neglect his prime responsibility to sustain morale. After the abortive battle of Valutina on 19 August, he visited the 127th Regiment on the battlefield, which was still

---

* Gareis, *Kampf und Ende der 98 Infanterie-Division*, quoted by Albert Seaton in *The Russo-German War 1941-45*.

littered with debris and corpses, to reward them with an eagle-standard which could only be won in action. Drawing them up in a square, he said to them with pardonable hyperbole,

This battle has been the most beautiful feat of arms in our history. You are men with whom one could conquer the world. The killed have achieved an immortal death. Here is your eagle. It will serve you as a rallying-point in moments of danger. Swear to me that you will never desert it, will always tread the path of honour, will defend our country and never allow France, our France, to be insulted.

There was a shouted reply: 'We swear it!' A Grenadier sergeant was then promoted lieutenant for his courage. The colonel of the regiment said the necessary words, but failed to embrace him. 'Well, Colonel, the accolade! The accolade!' said Napoleon sharply. At another review on the same day, a commanding officer mentioned to the Emperor the names of half-a-dozen officers who had distinguished themselves. 'How is it, Colonel?' said Napoleon. 'Are all your soldiers cowards then?' – and he called from the ranks the non-commissioned-officers and men who deserved promotion, inviting their comrades to nominate them. It was said by Ségur that 'he transformed the field of death into a field of triumph'. His manner, imperial yet paternal, his promise that news of their achievements would reach their families through his despatches, his assumption that they shared his ambition, were exhilarating, at least temporarily, till heat and cold and hunger lowered their spirits once again.

At his headquarters he saw no reason to impair his health for the sake of proving that he could share his men's privations. His personal train consisted in eight canteen waggons, a carriage for his wardrobe, two butlers, two valets, three cooks, four footmen and eight grooms. He normally travelled in a coach drawn by six horses, but would ride for short distances and occasionally march. When in contact with the enemy, he would mount one of his chargers, of which his favourite was Marengo. At night, if no suitable house or monastery was found for him, he slept in his carriage on a makeshift couch, but more often in a tent, of which a reconstruction is displayed in the Musée de l'Armée in the

Invalides, ten-foot square, equipped with a folding camp-bed, chair and table. A sword lay always within his reach. He ate frugally but well. He never lacked supplies of his special Chambertin.

He worked all day, even in motion, for his carriage was fitted with a desk and lights, and Berthier was always at his side to take dictated orders to the corps commanders or the most distant parts of the Empire. Berthier executed his instructions with utter devotion, resolute in spite of Napoleon's unmerited reproaches and frequent changes of mind, and, when asked, would give his opinion frankly. The two of them were attended by a cloud of aides-de-camp, all men of aristocratic birth ('One might imagine oneself in Paris,' wrote one of them, Fezensac), whose duties in normal circumstances were light, in battle highly dangerous, for it was their task to carry messages to different parts of the field. In addition, there was a crowd of functionaries. Fezensac thought the headquarters too elaborate. When Berthier reviewed it at Vilna, 'from a distance one could have mistaken it for a Brigade drawn up for battle.... This immense administrative corps was almost useless from the very beginning of the campaign, and became actually an impediment [*nuisible*] later.' The entire staff required fifty-two carriages, innumerable carts, and 650 horses to transport them.

As the army advanced towards Moscow, they were not much troubled by the partisans who became so serious a menace during the retreat. They were not yet organized, and the Russian nobility feared to put weapons into the hands of serfs, who might turn them against their masters. Why then – it is one of the most interesting questions raised by the campaign – did Napoleon not promise them their liberty? On his return to Paris in December 1812 he explained his reasons to the Senate: 'I could have armed the greater part of the population against the Tsar if I had proclaimed the freedom of the serfs. A great number of villages asked me for it. But when I got to know the brutishness of that very numerous class of Russian people, I refused to grant a measure which would have been a sentence of death to many families and consigned them to terrible torture.' While in Moscow, he gave another reason: that the serfs, who formed ninety per cent of the population, were already so incensed against the

French that he would have incurred 'all the odium of such a measure without reaping any benefit'. The peasants had been convinced by their priests that the French were immoral atheists who would ravish their wives and daughters, overthrow their ikons, and subject them to a servitude to which serfdom was very heaven in comparison. Besides, there were very few to whom Napoleon could have made his intention known. They had fled, or were forcibly evacuated, at his approach. But his main motive seems to have been that he thought emancipation of the serfs an unworthy method of warfare by one Emperor against another, or as Caulaincourt put it, 'unseemly in a monarch who, with reason, prided himself on having restored social order to Europe'. The consequent revolt would have been uncontrollable, the country delivered up to civil war, the nobility exterminated. How could Alexander ever be induced to make peace with Napoleon in such a situation? The Polish nobles, who also owned serfs, would abandon his cause.

The reasoning was sound, but the result disastrous for the French. In 1812, 190,000 serfs willingly joined the militia, thousands more the partisans. Only in three towns in Penza province was there a rising in favour of Napoleon, and it was quickly suppressed. The brutality of his reprisals against the partisans, as of the Wehrmacht's in the Ukraine, convinced the others that their emancipation from tyranny must come, if ever, from within. But how from within? If they hoped that by fighting so resolutely against Napoleon they might be rewarded with their liberty, they were disappointed. Alexander's manifesto to his people in 1814 included just one line of gratitude, 'The peasants, our loyal people, will be recompensed by God.'

Although the maps were poor, Napoleon could tell from them the names of the next villages and the courses of the major streams. This was fortunate, because he could obtain no information from inhabitants or prisoners, for there were none. The retreating army had removed even the signposts. They destroyed the bridges and fired the towns. The French pillaged what was left, and Napoleon made another futile gesture to restrain them, as at Vitebsk. He said that looters would be shot without trial. But when a man was brought before him and sank to his knees to implore forgiveness, holding up a child which he pretended was his own, Napoleon, indifferent more than touched, let him go free. As they approached Viasma on 28 August, he hoped to save the town by rushing it. It, too, was soon in flames. The army found almost nothing there, but Napoleon, with an eye on Parisian morale, wrote from Viasma to Marie-Louise, 'I am in a rather handsome city. There are thirty churches, 15,000 inhabitants, and many shops with vodka and other useful objects for the soldiers.' In fact, the further they advanced, the more complete the flight of the people and the greater the devastation. Not even old people or the sick remained.

Two days later he continued by forced marches to Gzatsk. The rain had now turned the tracks into quagmires, and a night's bivouac was as tiring as a day's march. Napoleon himself was affected by it. He told his doctor Mestivier, 'I am getting old. My legs are swollen and I have difficulty in passing water. It is no doubt the dampness of these bivouacs, for I depend on my skin for my life.' His pulse was irregular, his cough dry. His illness lasted until, and beyond, Borodino.

One small incident raised his spirits. Six miles short of Gzatsk, Murat captured a Cossack and a negro cook. Napoleon interviewed both. The negro asked to whom he was speaking, and when told that it was the Emperor in person, at first refused to believe it, and when finally convinced, prostrated himself in front of him, then rose to his feet to sing and dance. The Cossack, an intelligent and quick-eyed man, told Napoleon that Kutuzov had assumed command, and that he intended to fight for Moscow. He complained bitterly of Barclay, who, he said, had prevented them from fighting at Vilna or Smolensk by shutting them up in towns instead of facing Napoleon in the open, adding that only the Cossacks were worthy of Russia. 'If Napoleon had Cossacks in his army, by this time he would be Emperor of China.' He continued, according to Caulaincourt, who was present throughout the interview, with these remarkable words:

If Moscow is taken and the French enter the Cossack country, Russia is lost. Cossacks will have done their duty to the very last, and then they will side with Napoleon. Napoleon is a great general; Alexander is a good Tsar. If he liked, Alexander could be the best general in Russia. Russian generals are too fond of their ease; they sleep too much; they must have cushions and every comfort; they only think of themselves, not of their soldiers' needs. The French fight well, but they do not keep a good lookout. They like to pillage; they slip away from their units to hunt through houses, and Cossacks profit by this and capture large numbers every day, and recover their booty from them. The Cossacks like the King of Naples [Murat], who makes a fine show, for he is a brave fellow and always the first to come under fire. Word has gone around that he is not to be killed, but they want to take him prisoner.

It was true about Murat. After Kutuzov's arrival to take command, the Cossacks became more active, and Murat was obliged to exhaust his cavalry against trivial opposition. He was always in the forefront, and his mien so fierce and contemptuous, theatrical and noble, that they would often retire, astonished, at the very sight of him.

Excited by the prospect of a battle, Napoleon ordered all unnecessary vehicles to be burnt to clear the road for the artillery, and offered to sacrifice his own carriage as an example. The order went unheeded. The whole vast column entered Gzatsk, where he received the news that the Russians were digging in thirty miles ahead, at Borodino.

In *War and Peace* Tolstoy speculates why the battle was fought at all. 'There was not the least sense in it. Its immediate result for the Russians was, and was bound to be, that we were brought a step further towards the destruction of Moscow, and for the French that they were brought nearer the destruction of their whole army.' The argument is typically paradoxical. Neither side was 'bound to' win or lose. They were almost equally matched; if Kutuzov was slightly weaker in numbers, he had the advantage of prepared positions and stronger artillery. If Napoleon was the better general, his genius was not displayed at its best on that day. The 'sense in it' for the French was that they needed a major battle and could not avoid it; for the Russians that they were making a last-ditch stand to save their capital. If Napoleon won, he might capture Moscow, but would not have conquered

Russia. If Kutuzov won, the Grand Army would reel back to Smolensk in greater safety than in fact they did from Moscow. There was an imperative reason for both to fight, and the outcome was in doubt not only at the end of the day, but 173 years later. The most one can say in support of Tolstoy's paradox is that the battle was a tactical victory for Napoleon which led to his strategical defeat, but there was no inevitability about either.

Borodino lies seventy miles west of Moscow. When Tolstoy visited the battlefield, he covered the distance in a single day. Today it can be done in two hours. It is a small village on the 'new road' from Smolensk, which deviates slightly at this point from the 'old road' which runs parallel to it about two miles to the south. The Koloch, a tributary of the River Moskva, is crossed by the new road a short distance from the village, and two streams enter it from north and south at about the same point (see page 73). The ground between the two roads, where the major action took place, is gently undulating, with about the same rise and fall as the field of Waterloo, but cut by gullies and watercourses, none of them a sufficient obstacle to prevent the free movement of cavalry or horse-drawn artillery except the ravine of the Koloch, which is steep and wooded, though in several places fordable. The battlefield was open farmland from which the corn had just been harvested, interspersed with small spinneys of birch and fir, and a quite dense forest behind the Russian position. A few hamlets – Schevardino, Semionovskaya and Utitsa – speckled the plain. Its appearance today is altered by enlarged woodlands (the panorama by Jean-Charles Langlois in the Musée de l'Armée, Paris, shows how comparatively treeless it was), memorial buildings and concrete emplacements of World War II (the battlefield is a palimpsest of two wars), but it is readily intelligible as the site where Kutuzov, or his military secretary, Toll, chose to make his stand. By chance it had been the boyhood home of Colonel Davidov, Bagration's aide-de-camp and later the leader of the Russian partisans, and he knew every fold in the ground.

Kutuzov deployed his forces at an obtuse angle. His right wing, commanded by Barclay, guarded the crossings of the Koloch, his left the old Smolensk–Moscow road. Borodino village was the hinge, held by the Chasseurs of the Russian Im-

perial Guard. The centre, under Bagration, lay along a low ridge
below Semionovskaya, and on it he constructed two earth fortifications, a redoubt known to history as the Great or Raevski's
Redoubt after its commander, and to its left three mutually sup-
porting batteries, called the *flèches*, two in front and one in rear,
held by Borozdin's corps. Kutuzov also ordered the construction
of a third bastion, a mile ahead on a flattened knoll, the Schevardino Redoubt, an outpost which was to be held long enough
to give him time to complete the defence-works on the ridge.

The Russian position was as strong as any which could be
found in flattish country that lacked any major obstacle, and
Bennigsen's criticism that 'it was protected by wretched little
rivers, fordable anywhere, leaving both wings open and relying
on a few earthworks hurriedly thrown up' was an overstatement
by a man who was heavily prejudiced against any decision made
by Kutuzov; in the event Napoleon was unable to exploit its
weaknesses, so the battle developed into a trial of mutual slaughter that could have taken place almost anywhere. By holding the
slightly higher ground Kutuzov could dominate the battlefield
with his artillery. He had a forest behind him to conceal and
manoeuvre his reserves. He had a ravine to guard his right wing,
and swampy woods his left. The ground in front was broken. He
straddled the two roads to Moscow. His disadvantages were that
his army was spread over five miles while Napoleon might concentrate his on two, and that his left wing, held more weakly,
might give way. The issue depended upon the focus of the
French attack, and whether Kutuzov would be quick enough
and mobile enough to repel it. He might have placed too many
divisions in the north, where they would be wasted if not engaged. Could he switch them in time to the south if the attack
came there? That was his only possible manoeuvre from prepared positions. He could use Barclay's army, unless it were
directly attacked, as a vast reserve to reinforce his centre, the
Great Redoubt and the *flèches*. These had been conceived mainly
as artillery fulcrums, but they could, and did, become centres of
infantry and cavalry resistance too.

When Napoleon arrived within sight of the battlefield on 5
September, he saw immediately that the Schevardino redoubt
must be captured to clear his approaches to the main Russian

line. It was a pentagon formed by breastworks pierced with embrasures for twelve guns, and all around it stood the infantry, under Prince Gorchakov, in tight ranks to a distance of several hundred yards from the redoubt itself. Napoleon began his attack at 4 pm with cavalry, and when they were repulsed by Russian cannon-fire, he sent in Compans's division, which captured the redoubt within an hour. The Russians retook it with heavy casualties, and before dark it had changed hands four times. A Spanish regiment eventually remained in possession, and the Russian outpost became the French. The carnage on each side had been dreadful. The French and allies lost 2,000 men. Every Russian fought till killed by the bayonet. There were no prisoners.

On 6 September the two armies moved into their preparatory positions. It was said that only a single musket shot was fired that day, as if both sides, conscious of what was coming, observed an undeclared truce. Napoleon was making his reconnaissance, riding along the whole line from left to right. Davout advised a wide outflanking movement with 40,000 men, beyond the Utitsa woods, to come on Bagration from behind, but Napoleon replied that it would weaken his main front and the manoeuvre might cause the whole Russian line to retreat before he could come to grips with them. He was determined on a battle of attrition, a brutal mauling encounter, like El Alamein, which would rely heavily on artillery at the start and end with the piercing of the Russian centre by his infantry. He placed his three infantry corps, Ney's, Junot's and Davout's, opposite the earthworks on a front of one and a half miles south of the Koloch. Eugène's corps and Grouchy's cavalry were north of it facing Borodino village. Poniatowski was on the old road to the south. The Guard and Murat's cavalry were held in reserve near the Schevardino redoubt, and Napoleon set up his battle headquarters on a lower mound two hundred yards north-east of it, where today stands the only French memorial on the battlefield. The redoubt itself, which would have provided better observation, was too cluttered with dead and wounded to be tolerable throughout a long day.

In round figures (Chandler's) Napoleon had at his disposal just over 100,000 infantry, 28,000 cavalry and 590 guns. Kutuzov

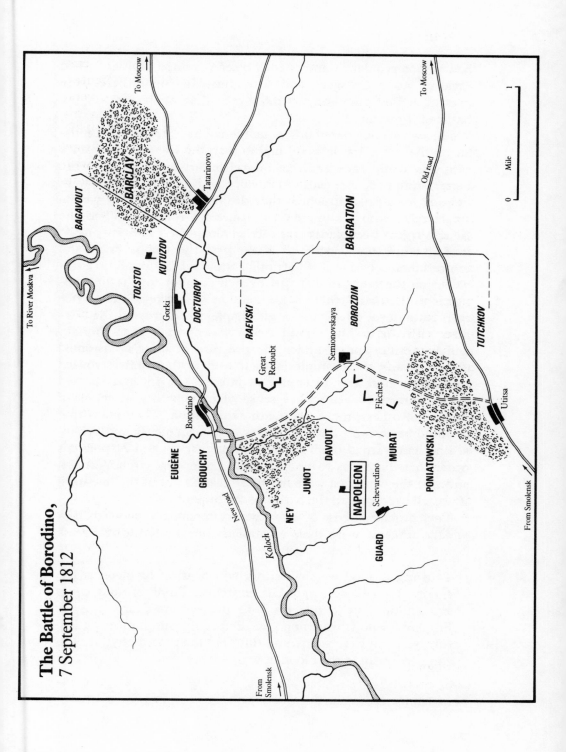

The Battle of Borodino,
7 September 1812

To Moscow

To River Moskva

BAGAVOUT

BARCLAY

Tatarinovo

To Moscow

Old road

KUTUZOV

TOLSTOI

Gorki

DOCTUROV

RAEVSKI

Great
Redoubt

BAGRATION

BORODZIN

Semionovskaya

TUTCHKOV

Utitsa

Borodino

Flèches

New road

EUGÈNE

GROUCHY

Koloch

NEY

JUNOT

DAVOUT

MURAT

NAPOLEON

Schevardino

PONIATOWSKI

GUARD

From
Smolensk

From Smolensk

0   Mile   1

had 72,000 regular infantry, 10,000 semi-trained militia, 17,000 cavalry, 7,000 Cossacks and 640 guns. In total, there were present at Borodino 100,000 more men than at the start of the battle of Waterloo.

The two armies were fairly equally matched, but Russian morale on the eve of battle stood higher than the French. Kutuzov's men were comparatively fresh and well-nourished, and they were better equipped, especially in cavalry and artillery. They were fighting for a cause in which they deeply believed. They were a single race, with a common language and religion. When the Black Virgin of Smolensk was carried along their lines by priests in full vestments waving their censers, the troops knelt and crossed themselves with a patriotic ecstasy which found no equivalent on the other side. In all French accounts of the preliminaries to the battle, there is no mention of any religious service or private devotion. Not a single chaplain had crossed the Niemen with them. The Grand Army was cynical, tired, hungry and homesick, and if under the pressure of their accustomed discipline and the example of their leaders the soldiers roused themselves next day to spurts of intense activity and showed great courage, it was with a sense of inevitability in some, of despair in others, more than with exhilaration. They knew that it would be an exceptionally bloody battle. Smolensk and Schevardino had warned them of Russian pugnacity, and Napoleon's order that there was to be no retreat under any circumstances, and that the wounded were not to be carried out of the line until it was all over, chilled the hearts of the bravest.

The proclamations of the two commanders showed how widely different were their emotional appeals. Kutuzov's read:

Trusting in God we shall either win or die. Napoleon is His enemy. He will desecrate His churches. Think of your wives and children, who rely on your protection. Think of your Emperor, who is watching you. Before the sun has set tomorrow, you will have written on this field the record of your faith and patriotism in the blood of your enemy.

Napoleon's read:

This is the battle you have so long desired! Now victory depends on you. We have need of it. Victory will give us abundance of supplies, good winter quarters and a prompt return to our motherland. Conduct yourselves as you did at Austerlitz, Friedland, Vitebsk and Smolensk. Let distant posterity say of each of you, 'He was present at the great battle beneath the walls of Moscow!'

That night, 6/7 September, Napoleon slept little. He watched anxiously the camp-fires on the Russian ridge, listened for the calls of their sentries, and sent repeatedly for assurance that they were not slipping away. In the evening he had received despatches containing the unwelcome news of Marmont's defeat by Wellesley at Salamanca on 22 July, and was consoled only by letters from Marie-Louise and the portrait of their little son, the King of Rome, by François Gérard, which he placed, pathetically, outside his tent to encourage any officer or man who passed by. Ségur described his mood as 'emotional, apprehensive', and he was feeling ill. His bladder was giving him renewed trouble, and he had a heavy cold. He worked with Berthier for a few hours, dosing himself with frequent sips of punch. Towards dawn he sent for his ADC, Jean Rapp. 'Well, Rapp, do you think we shall have a successful day?' 'There is no doubt about it, Sire. We have used up all our resources, and simply have to win. But it will be very bloody.' 'I know, but I have 80,000 men' (mentally he was already reserving the Guard). 'I shall lose 20,000, and with 60,000 I shall enter Moscow. There we shall be joined by reinforcements and be stronger than before the battle.' A little later he added, 'What is war? A barbaric profession, of which the only art is to be stronger at a given place.'

At 5.30 am he rode to his command-post near Schevardino, as his troops moved into line. They were dressed by his order in their *grande tenue* to add glory to their exploits and make the officers more easily distinguishable through the smoke. The battle was fought, on both sides, in a blaze of colour and flashing breastplates. The dawn was misty, but the sun ('the sun of Austerlitz' he exclaimed) soon broke through and the day remained fine till evening.

The battle began at 6 am with an absurd anti-climax. The

main French batteries had been sited out of range, and after firing a few rounds which fell short, the guns were limbered up to move closer to the Russian lines. Then simultaneously Eugène's Corps attacked the village of Borodino, Davout began his first attack on Bagration's *flèches*, and Poniatowski advanced on Utitsa. On the left the attack at first went well. Delzons captured the village within fifteen minutes, and swept the Russian Guard aside to seize the bridge over the Koloch. They were already within a few hundred yards of the Great Redoubt, which lay up a gentle slope from the stream. For a moment it seemed that Eugène's and Grouchy's diversion (as Napoleon had intended it) might seize the nodal point in the Russian defences, but a counter-attack forced them back over the river, and they were held there for the rest of the morning. On the right flank the Poles, out of sight in the woods and almost out of contact with Napoleon, soon captured Utitsa, but were prevented by Tutchkov from outflanking the main line. No serious threat developed there. Utitsa remained a sideshow, thought to be so little relevant to the main battle that today it forms no part of the battlefield tour allowed to visitors.

The struggle, all day, was in the centre. Davout attacked the *flèches* frontally under an arch of intense cannon-fire from both sides. When the survivors came to fight hand-to-hand, their fear and anger rendered them mutually merciless. Both sides hurriedly reinforced, Kutuzov by moving down part of Tolstoi's and Bagavout's corps (now that he saw no further threat from Eugène on that flank) to help Borozdin, and Napoleon part of the cavalry and Ney's corps to help Davout. Montbrun, in command of the cavalry, was killed. Davout was wounded. So were Dessaix and Compans, the hero of Schevardino. Next fell Rapp, whom Napoleon had sent to replace Compans: it was his twenty-second wound in the Emperor's service. A few yards of ground were gained alternately by each side at appalling cost. For half an hour the French held one of the three *flèches*, but were driven out. Attacking again, Ney gained two of them, and the third was over-run when the Russian 7th Grenadier Division defending it had virtually ceased to exist. Bagration himself was wounded in the leg, carried off the field, and died of an infection seventeen days later. His loss was a critical blow to the Russian army.

This was still not the end of the battle for the *flèches*. These open emplacements, constructed of earth ramparts reinforced on the inner side with wattle hurdles and pierced by gun-embrasures at intervals of twenty yards, changed hands again and again. Corpses piled up to form ramps for both attack and defence. Napoleon committed 45,000 men against this single point and bombarded it with 400 guns. The cavalry was flung in to join the infantry, but uselessly, because the confusion, the broken ground and the congestion impeded all free movement. It was a matter of struggling for a foothold in a ditch or between fallen men and horses, crouching under an upturned cannon, watching for the fall of shot, glimpsing suddenly a contorted face that could be friend or foe, a spasmodic thrust of the bayonet (for there was no space to fire nor time to reload), continuous noise, terror and murder without relief for five hours. Was this 'the battle you have so long desired'? The 'achievement' of which posterity would tell?

At about midday the Russians abandoned the *flèches* and the ruins of Semionovskaya, and retreated a few hundred yards. When the French colonel who had commanded the final assault began to retreat again, Murat rushed to him, demanding to know the reason. The colonel indicated the mass of corpses and the cannonade which was adding dozens to them every minute. 'You see that I cannot stay here.' 'Then I'll stay,' said Murat, and rallied the troops.

The Russians still held the Great Redoubt. Foreseeing that Napoleon would make his next major effort against it, Kutuzov ordered a demonstration on his right flank, around Borodino village, which the French still held, to threaten their rear. He sent Platov with his Cossacks and Uvarov's 1st Cavalry Corps, some 8,000 horse in all, across the Koloch two miles downstream from Borodino, hoping that their sudden appearance would cause consternation among the French. It did. The attack was not pressed home, possibly because cavalry in isolation cannot sustain an attack against compact infantry, but the movement was menacing enough to weaken Napoleon's momentum and delay for an hour his assault on the Redoubt.

This was the climax of the battle and its best remembered incident. The Redoubt, which was reconstructed in the mid-nineteenth century by Tsar Nicholas I when Bagration's tomb (the most moving, because the simplest, of the battlefield memorials) was laid centrally within it, was a natural knoll fortified by Raevski's division on three sides by the same thick, revetted earthworks as the *flèches*. The defences were as primitive, and as effective, as those of an Iron Age fort. The approach from the west was uphill, fairly steep at this point and made more difficult by a ditch and fox-holes dug outside the ramparts. Essentially it was an artillery position dominating the plain, and there was room inside it for twenty guns and little more than a battalion of infantry, who fired across the ramparts between the gun-emplacements. Its weakness was its east side, where the ground was flatter and left open to permit the entry of guns, men and horses from the Russian rear.

Since Eugène's attack in the early morning, the Redoubt had been under intense bombardment. Now was the moment to assault it frontally by a combined infantry and cavalry attack. Eugène's corps of three divisions was to cross the river and ascend the slope, forcing an entrance into the Redoubt by the gun-embrasures while six horsed regiments turned it on the right as if making for the Russian cavalry in the rear, and then wheeled inwards to attack the Redoubt from behind. The command of the cavalry was given to Napoleon's aide-de-camp Auguste de Caulaincourt, brother of the Master of Horse. The infantry attack succeeded at almost the same moment as Caulaincourt broke through in the opposite direction. The Russian gunners met them with hand-spikes and ramrods, and not one of them survived. Caulaincourt, at the head of the 5th Cuirassiers, fell at the moment of his triumph, struck through the heart by a bullet as he forced the open flank. 'He died as a brave man should,' said Napoleon, when told the news, 'that is in deciding the battle.' Turning to Caulaincourt's brother, and seeing tears in his eyes, he offered him the chance to retire. Caulaincourt 'merely lifted his hat slightly as a token of his gratitude, and refused' (Ségur).

If Napoleon considered the battle 'decided', he was almost the only one who did so. He was now in possession of the whole enemy front line, from Borodino to Utitsa, and his artillery occupied the *flèches*. But the Russians had retreated only a few hundred yards to form a new front. This was Napoleon's opportunity to use his remaining reserve, the Old Guard, to complete the victory. The troops who had already been engaged were too exhausted to attempt it. Time and again during the morning, his Marshals had begged him to deploy the Guard, but Napoleon had consistently refused, at first because he must preserve it intact to meet a flank attack like Platov's, and later saying that it would be madness to risk his finest and only uncommitted formation when, for all he could foresee, another battle for Moscow might be necessary. 'When you have come 800 leagues from France, you do not wreck your last reserve,' he said to Rapp. 'I am certain to win the battle without it.'

Was he right? There must remain a doubt whether the Guard would have broken through. They failed to do so at Waterloo, at an equivalent phase of the battle, but there the British squares stood in their original positions. At Borodino the Russians were now on unprepared ground and desperately attempting to restore order. They had no more reserves of their own. A successful attack by 20,000 fresh troops, the élite of the Grand Army, could have had a devastating effect. However, even if the victory had been overwhelming, it would have led to the same result, the capture of Moscow, and a new Russian army would soon have been formed behind it. The Guard, in fact, was never used *en masse* during the campaign. It fought on the way back at Krasnoe, but by then the retreat had diminished it to a ghost of its former self. This could not be foreseen. So, apart from a few battalions of the Young Guard and its artillery which entered the battle spasmodically, the Imperial Guard remained all day behind Schevardino, playing its regimental marches.

It is sometimes alleged that Napoleon's refusal to commit the Guard indicates a lapse from his old energy, and for other reasons too his men thought his behaviour at Borodino was flaccid. His plan of attack had been unimaginative. He had stationed himself all day a mile from the fighting, watching it through a spy-glass and sending orders which were based on inaccurate information or arrived too late to be executed. At no stage did he galvanize his battalions by his actual presence. One of his front-line officers, Colonel Lejeune, later said, 'We were all surprised not to find the energetic man of Marengo and Austerlitz', and Ségur that 'he displayed a hesitation hitherto unknown in him. ... Everyone around him regarded him with astonishment.' Ney, on receiving a message that the Emperor was hesitating because 'he could not clearly see the chessboard', exploded with anger: 'Have we come so far simply to possess a battlefield? What is he doing so far back? There he hears of our reverses, not of our successes. He's not a General any more: he's an Emperor. Let him return to the Tuileries and leave the fighting to us.'

Few realized that Napoleon was sick. His cold lowered his vitality and his bladder infection made it difficult for him to ride. Lejeune put it delicately: 'This type of illness made it impossible for him to act solely in the interests of his glory.' It must also be acknowledged that in so intense a battle the commander's own safety is of supreme importance and that he must remain where he could easily be found. He was not out of range. Several times his staff begged him to withdraw further back, but he refused, ignoring cannon balls that rolled, it was said, to his very feet. He was equally indifferent to his comforts. Twice he angrily refused food, but towards the end of the day accepted a glass of Chambertin and a slice of bread. Then, at last, he mounted his horse and rode to Semionovskaya, from where he surveyed the Russian lines. He saw that they were unbroken; that they might even be forming up to attack again.

After the capture of the Redoubt at about 3.30 pm, the battle slowly died down except for cannon-fire and an abortive attempt by Grouchy's cavalry to find an exploitable gap. The French artillery cut down thousands of Russian infantry, who died where they stood, but there was no counter-attack. On the far right of the French line Poniatowski captured from the militia a rounded hill east of Utitsa. This was the last, inconclusive action of the day. In these final moments, Napoleon offered to send in the Young Guard, but now it was Murat who protested. It was too late in the day, he said, and a renewal of the battle on so small a scale would mean further sacrifice with no great result. Only the entire Imperial Guard could make any difference, and Napoleon would still not consent to use it. As dusk fell, the two armies rested half a mile apart.

Who had won? Both commanders claimed the victory. Kutuzov's official despatch announced 'the defeat of Bonaparte in a

great battle', and when it was read out in the Church of
Alexander Nevsky in St Petersburg, there was great rejoicing. In
his private report to the Tsar he was more guarded. The Russian
losses had been heavy, but the French had lost many more. 'Our
batteries were captured, then recaptured, but in the end the
enemy did not gain an inch of ground. But Your Majesty will
understand that after a battle of such intensity, the line held by
us at the start was too long for our reduced forces to hold, so I
decided, after passing the night on the battlefield, to withdraw
six versts.' Napoleon wrote to Marie-Louise: 'I write to you
from the battlefield of Borodino. Yesterday I beat the Russians.
Their whole army, 120,000 strong, was there. The battle was a
hot one. Victory was ours at two in the afternoon. I took several
thousand prisoners and sixty cannon. Their losses can be estimated at 30,000 men. I lost many killed and wounded. My health
is good, the weather a little fresh.'

In fact, the losses on each side were crippling to both. Figures
vary, but the Russians had lost about 44,000 killed and wounded,
one in every three of their men engaged, the French at least
35,000, including forty-three generals. Instead of 'several thousand prisoners', Napoleon had captured about 700. Instead of
'sixty cannon', only twenty, all smashed. At St Helena Napoleon
called it 'the most terrible of my battles, in which the French
showed themselves worthy of victory, and the Russians of being
invincible'. Only at Wagram had the total casualties been so
great, and that was a battle decisively won. Napoleon could claim
that at Borodino he remained at nightfall in occupation of the
battlefield, that his Guard was intact, and that as a direct result
of the battle he entered Moscow. But victory in his experience
meant that the enemy must be seen to have been routed, thousands of prisoners captured, a mass of trophies taken, and that
negotiations for an armistice, if not surrender, must follow. None
of this applied to Borodino. Kutuzov could claim that he withdrew 80,000 men in good order and in his own time, that he still
barred the road to Moscow, and that his army had displayed
such exemplary courage that the battle became, and remains
today, a symbol of their national spirit. To call it a drawn battle
would be to err in Russia's favour. The official guide to the
battlefield describes it as 'a great strategic victory, because it

achieved Kutuzov's aim, to change the balance in favour of the Russians', and although this can be argued in the longer term, a more impartial verdict must be that for Napoleon it was a marginal victory on the field, and for Kutuzov 'the kind of victory', as Tolstoy said, 'that compels the enemy to recognize the moral superiority of his opponent'. De Maistre (quoted by Isaiah Berlin in *The Hedgehog and the Fox*) put it more succinctly: *'Qu'est ce qu'une bataille perdue? C'est une bataille qu'on croit avoir perdue.'* The Russians did not consider that they had lost Borodino.

As night descended on 7 September there was no elation in the French camp. Everyone noticed that Napoleon looked worried and exhausted. To his entourage he said encouragingly that peace lay in Moscow: 'When the great nobles of Russia see us masters of their capital, they will think twice about fighting on.' But to Berthier he said in great privacy that all those men had been killed to no purpose. There should have been more prisoners. The Russian spirit was not broken. He could see their camp-fires 1,000 yards ahead, and hear their shouts of 'Victory!' As he toured the battlefield, he commented on the endurance of the Russian wounded, who were kissing the image of St Nicholas to help them forget their pain. When a horse stepped on one of them and the man cried aloud, an aide said, 'It's only a Russian.' 'After a victory,' Napoleon replied, 'there are no enemies, only men.' He was in a different mood than after Smolensk. He ordered the maimed of both sides to be carried back, most of them to the monastery of Kolotskoye, which was transformed into a fearful hospital. Dr Jean Larrey, the senior French surgeon, personally amputated 200 limbs, giving his patients a napkin to bite on and a quick gulp of brandy before the knife cut. The dead were left where they lay, and it was not until May 1813 that the peasants burnt or buried the last of the corpses.

Kutuzov was at first determined to renew the battle next day. He had played a personal part in the day's events little more glorious than Napoleon's. His men reproached him afterwards for remaining too far from the battlefield, beyond Gorki, where he could see little of what was going on, and except for moving his right wing gradually towards the centre and organizing Platov's abortive raid, he had made no decisions which influenced

Napoleon Bonaparte, after Gerard

Top left Bagration

Above right Alexander I of Russia

Above Kutuzov

The Battle of Borodino, 12 September

The attack on Smolensk in August

The council of war at Fili, 13
September: (*left to right*) Os-
termann Tolstoi, Kutuzov
(*seated*), Raevski, Konovnitsin,
Barclay de Tolly, Uvarov,
Docturov, Ermolov (*standing*),
Kaisarov and Bennigsen

Count Rostopchin, Governor
of Moscow, 1812

Moscow in flames: the Kremlin (*left*) overlooking the River Moskva

The beginning of the retreat

During the retreat, French troops fighting off the Cossacks

The crossing of the Beresina, drawn at the time by an unknown artist

The final stages of the retreat

the battle, in contrast to Bagration, its hero, and Barclay, who had risked his life again and again almost as if he did not expect to survive it. When told that they had lost all their front-line positions, Kutuzov refused to believe it. 'I am in the best position to know how the battle went,' he shouted. 'The French attacks have been successfully repulsed everywhere, and tomorrow I shall put myself at the head of the army and drive the enemy from the sacred soil of Russia.' But when asked by Colonel Wolzhogen, a Prussian officer on Barclay's staff, whether this was an order, Kutuzov directed that, if Napoleon did not attack on the morrow, the Russian army would not stir either. They would merely straighten their positions from Gorki to the old Smolensk road and hold them. Barclay sent back the message that this was impossible. The troops were too exhausted to resist a new attack, and too few of them were left to man so long a line. They were short of ammunition, and had had no food. Kutuzov accepted the inevitable at 3 am on 8 September, and ordered the withdrawal of the entire army to beyond Mojaisk. At dawn only a Cossack rearguard was visible to the French. This time Napoleon was heartened by the news that the Russians had gone. It confirmed his boast of victory, and he himself was in no fit state to fight a second day. Indeed, he was actually incapable of command. The strain, and his cold, had robbed him of his voice.

CHAPTER FIVE
MOSCOW

The seventy miles between Borodino and Moscow were covered by the two armies in a week, without a further battle. Napoleon himself, still speechless and obliged to write his orders, remained in Mojaisk for two days, 11 and 12 September, and sent Murat ahead in pursuit. The small town contained 3,000 Russian wounded, abandoned by their comrades as at Smolensk. They suffered terribly, bandaged with hay for lack of lint, and keeping themselves alive with the few grains they found in the straw they lay upon. Too weak to move the dead, they used the corpses as pillows, until the French threw them into the street to make room for their own weary bodies.

Colonel Fezensac, who took over command of an infantry regiment in Mojaisk, wrote that he was horrified by the exhaustion and numerical weakness of his men. The regiment retained only 900 out of the 2,800 who had crossed the Rhine:

> We had never suffered such losses. Never had the army's morale been so damaged. I no longer found the soldiers' old gaiety. A gloomy silence has replaced the songs and amusing stories which previously had helped them to forget the fatigues of the long marches. Even the officers appeared anxious, and they continued serving only from a sense of duty and honour. This depression, natural in a defeated army, was remarkable after a decisive action, after a victory which opened to us the gates of Moscow.

It was in this condition that they stumbled forward to their goal. The army was again divided into three columns on as wide a front as possible to gather food and fodder from the villages, but not so far apart as to risk separation and encirclement. They were now approaching the area where rich Muscovites had their country estates, and occasionally a battalion would find itself a night's billet of exceptional luxury. For most of them it was a march of painful slowness in ragged uniforms and boots worn to tatters, and no shelter at the day's end. The lack of any contact with the retreating Russians except by a rare skirmish was a cause of more anxiety than relief, for they might attack anywhere. Napoleon feared a wide outflanking movement through the enormous stretches of country on either side of him, and if it came to another battle he would be seriously short of ammunition, having fired 90,000 artillery rounds at Borodino alone. New supplies were not available this side of Minsk.

The Russians withdrew to Moscow uncertain what to do next. The decision was left to Kutuzov, as the Tsar, in St Petersburg, was too far away for consultation. Kutuzov's instinct was to fight for the city, but having retreated to its very suburbs he had a limited choice of ground, all of it unfavourable to the defence. If he abandoned Moscow to Napoleon without fighting, he would save the army and might ultimately gain an advantage, but the Tsar, army and people immediately, and history ultimately, might never forgive him. If he did retreat, in which direction should it be? East, towards Vladimir, where he would find boundless space to manoeuvre? South-east and south to Kolomna and Tula, where lay his main supplies? South-west to Kaluga, to threaten Napoleon's communications? Or north, to place a barrier between him and his next presumed objective, St Petersburg?

Kutuzov's headquarters were now at Fili, a village so close to Moscow's walls that the Kremlin is visible from its church-tower and today it is one of Moscow's western suburbs. His army occupied a front between Fili and the Sparrow Hills (see map page 87), one much narrower than Napoleon's three branching columns, which extended between the river Moskva and the Kaluga road. At any moment Kutuzov might be outflanked, just as Napoleon feared himself before he knew where Kutuzov was. He decided to take the advice of his generals, and summoned them to Fili on 13 September for the most important conference of the campaign. Its dramatization in *War and Peace* is a classic episode in the novel, but it is not quite accurate. Tolstoy was determined at that point in his story (he changed his view later) to represent Kutuzov as somnolent and vacillating. In fact he took the boldest decision of his career.

Kutuzov held two conferences at Fili on the afternoon of 13 September: one with Barclay and Rostopchin, Governor of Moscow, the second two hours later with nearly all the senior generals. At the first, Barclay began by urging retreat, and advised the Kaluga road, as all their supplies were based there. Rostopchin agreed, because their present positions sloped towards the city, and if they lost the battle, the army would be forced to retreat helter-skelter and would be broken up in the streets. He was careful to conceal from Kutuzov the assurances he had repeatedly given to the people of Moscow that the city would never be yielded. In his memoirs he contended that his half-hour talk with Kutuzov 'showed me the baseness, incapacity and cowardice of our army chief, to whom had been entrusted the salvation of our country.... My duty was over, my conscience clear, but sorrow overcame me.' This two-faced man emerges wretchedly from the whole incident. Wishing retrospectively to pose as Moscow's champion who was forced to leave it defenceless by a witless, heartless veteran soldier, he was at the time encouraging Kutuzov to retreat, the people to leave the city, and his servants to set it on fire. Barclay, too, was guarding his reputation. At one moment he said that 'the only thing I desire is to be killed if we are mad enough to fight here', and at the next that Kutuzov should take the offensive to destroy Napoleon's right wing. If the decision was to retreat, it would be with his reluctant consent: if to fight, he was suggesting a method almost impossible to execute.

When the full conference convened, all the commanders were present except Miloradovich, who was in charge of the rearguard. They gathered in the cabin of a peasant named Sevastyanov, which has been reconstructed as a memorial on the new Smolensk road. It is a wooden hut of two rooms, with a stove in the corner of one of them, where the council-of-war met. There was enough rough furniture to seat the eight senior generals, the lesser ones standing, round a table spread with maps. There are several ear-witness accounts of what was said, not all agreeing.

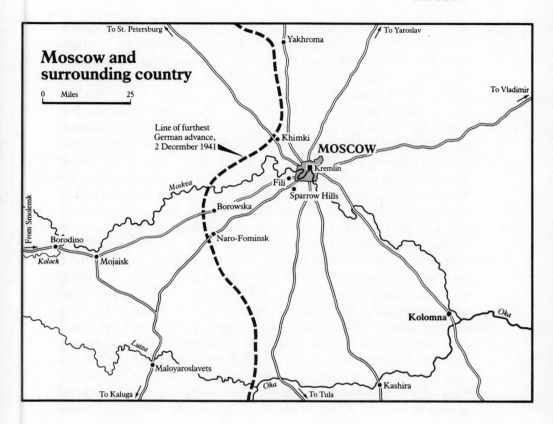

Moscow and surrounding country

0   Miles   25

Line of furthest
German advance,
2 December 1941

To St. Petersburg
Yakhroma
To Yaroslav
To Vladimir
Khimki
MOSCOW
Kremlin
Moskva
Fili
Sparrow Hills
Borowska
From Smolensk
Naro-Fominsk
Borodino
Koloch
Mojaisk
Oka
Kolomna
Luza
Maloyaroslavets
Oka
To Kaluga
To Tula
Kashira

But there is no doubt about the conclusion. Kutuzov opened the discussion by saying that as long as the army existed and was in a fit condition to fight, there was hope of winning the war, but if the army was destroyed, Moscow and Russia would perish – a statement which showed which way his mind had tended since the afternoon. Then he sat back to listen. Ermolov, who had been sent to inspect the Fili-Sparrow Hills position, reported that it was untenable. All agreed except Bennigsen, who had chosen it, but when he found no supporters, he adopted Barclay's alternative proposal, to attack Napoleon's right flank. This, too, was generally held to be impossible, for they had only 70,000 men against 100,000, and it would be too risky a manoeuvre to

87

shift masses of troops from right to left under the enemy's nose. Bennigsen retorted that it would be equally dangerous to withdraw the army through the city with the enemy on its heels. A retreat would result in the collapse of public confidence in their leaders. How could the people continue to believe that Borodino was a victory (as they had been told) if its consequence was the surrender of Moscow? His arguments convinced Docturov, Uvarov and Ermolov, according to Bennigsen's subsequent and biased account, but Barclay, wavering again, was in favour of retreat, and so were Raevski and Tolstoi. They knew that Eugène was already turning their right flank, and during the conference itself they heard that Poniatowski was threatening their left flank too. The sounds of fighting penetrated the thin walls.

The council-of-war was deeply divided, as much between shame and honour as on tactics. They looked to Kutuzov for a decision. He ordered a retreat. 'You are afraid of falling back through Moscow,' he said, 'but I consider it the only way of saving the army. Napoleon is a torrent which we are as yet unable to stem. Moscow will be the sponge that will suck him dry.' The army was to move that very night through the city and take the Kolomna road south-east, where it would find more abundant supplies and leave Napoleon guessing its future intentions. A few half-hearted protests were made that, if they had to retreat, it should be northwards, to protect St Petersburg, but Napoleon would be unlikely to embark upon a 350-mile march in winter to capture it, and it was a risk they must take. Kutuzov's decision on this point was perhaps more unexpected than his surrender of Moscow, but it was accepted by all the senior officers present.

In 1941 the Russians faced the same threat, but responded more heroically. On the sketch-map (p. 87) is marked the line of the furthest German advance. At Borodino, Mojaisk and Maloyaroslavets there had been battles of great intensity, and the Russians were pushed back almost to the city's outskirts. Zhukov, in command of the Moscow front, organized a quarter of a million citizens, seventy-five per cent of them women, to dig trenches and anti-tank ditches round the perimeter, and all the bridges, including those within Moscow itself, were prepared for demolition. The Government was ready, if necessary, to leave for Kuibyshev. Zukhov ordered spoiling attacks all along the front, declaring that 'there can be no falling back. There is no other place to fall back to.' Von Kluge was attacking north from Naro-Fominsk, Guderian towards Kashira. North-west of Moscow a detachment of the 2nd Panzer Division pushed into Khimki, an outer suburb within fifteen miles of the Kremlin, and German guns were moved up to shell the city. On 2 December the line was stabilized at every point, and the successful Soviet counter-attack began on 6 December, the day before Pearl Harbor.

Of course there were great differences between these two most critical moments in Moscow's history. The forces involved in 1941 were infinitely larger, and the front was as wide as the country itself. The Wehrmacht was stuck in mud, then snow, while Napoleon, arriving before Moscow nearly two months earlier in the year, still enjoyed fine weather. In 1941 Moscow was the capital city of Russia and its loss would have been a calamity; in 1812 it was St Petersburg. But the comparison between the two campaigns is still worth making. Zukhov and Stalin could have decided, like Kutuzov, that the sacrifice of Moscow would only postpone their ultimate victory, and indeed make it more probable, by drawing the Germans far beyond their means of supply. Instead, they decided to fight, if needs be within the city itself. It was a decision that turned the course of the Second World War, as Kutuzov's did that of 1812. From opposite ends – weakness and lack of will in 1812; courage and determination in 1941 – they achieved the same result.

In the army, as the news of Kutuzov's decision spread, there was intense dismay. Miloradovich appealed under a flag of truce to Sebastiani of the 2nd Cavalry Corps for a few hours' grace to evacuate the wounded and allow the Russians to retreat. If it was refused, the city would be burnt. Napoleon agreed without hesitation, more dazzled by the prospect of entering Moscow unopposed than tempted to attack the enemy when they were unprepared. All through the night of 13/14 September and the following day, the Russian army marched through the city in good order, and continued another twelve miles beyond it. Rostopchin's last act before joining them was to order the release of all the criminals in the prisons. Among them was a Russian traitor, and a Frenchman. The Russian was executed publicly, while the Frenchman looked on in terror. Rostopchin turned to him: 'You are French. You can welcome your compatriots. Tell them that Russia has only one traitor, and that you have just seen him die.'

Moscow was a city of 250,000 inhabitants, spread widely by its gardens and orchards to a circuit of twenty-five miles, the great stone palaces of the nobility, like Tolstoy's Rostovs, alternating with single-storey wooden cabins and huge bazaars. Its streets still retained their medieval inconsequence, and its character, in contrast to St Petersburg's, was easy-going and a bit dishevelled. There was a frivolity about the place, a cheerful cohabitation of rich and poor, tradesmen and gentry, peasants and artisans. A family of eight could have fifty rooms, or inhabit a single one. The nobility would also have a great estate outside the city, like Arkangelskoye, the property of Prince Yusupov, Palladian in architectural inspiration, almost wholly French in contents, and dependent upon 10,000 serfs. Moscow was cosmopolitan, but was also intensely Russian, with its six cathedrals and 1,500 churches of a peculiarly outlandish design, clusters of gilded belfries and coloured spiralling domes like huge turbans (Napoleon called them 'mosques'), which gave the city an Asiatic aspect, even a touch of Disneyland, in contrast to the westernized palaces of its chief inhabitants. Batiushkov in his *Walk through Moscow* (1812) spoke of this 'marvellous, outrageous, gigantic whole', the holiest city in Russia, but also its chief centre of commerce and Society.

This Society, until 1812, was Francophile. French was their normal language, and French plays and opera their most popular entertainment. They could have remained in the city to accept French occupation, as Parisians remained in Paris in 1870 and 1940, but they chose to abandon their homes to inevitable pillage, a demonstration of national pride and unity unparalleled in history. The flight had begun in August when the news of the fall of Smolensk reached them, and accelerated after Borodino, proof that the 'victory' and Rostopchin's promises were not believed. The first to leave were women and children, and carts bearing the treasures of the churches, but at this stage it was not a mass exodus – the nobility were hissed at the gates for cowardice and treachery. Then it became general. The evacuation by the common people was on foot, cart, or horseback, cows led behind, chickens crated, the children crying or thinking it an adventure, babies smiling their way through the humiliations of helplessness. They dispersed in every direction except west. Their motives were mixed. Partly they left because Rostopchin now ordered them to, partly from patriotism, but mainly because they expected from the French all the brutalities of an invading army and had heard the rumour that Moscow would be set on fire. If they stayed, they might lose everything, including their lives. If they fled, they might salvage something and one day return. Only 25,000 remained when the French entered the city, and they were people of the lowest class, foreigners, the criminals, and thousands of Russian sick and wounded.

Napoleon had spent the night of 13 September thirty miles from Moscow in a palace near Borowska belonging to Prince Galitzin, the 'first decent lodging' he had found since entering Russia. On the 14th he rode forward to the city, first in his coach, then on his horse Emir, and at 2 pm caught sight of it from a low rise known as Poklonnaya Gora, or Salutation Hill, where returning Muscovites would pause to do reverence. He then rode to Sparrow Hill, now the site of Moscow University, from where the view across the Moskva towards the Kremlin was even more spectacular. He stood there, scanning the myriad domes, spires and gilded palaces below him, and through his spy-glass saw a long black column coiling out of the distant gates. 'A cry of happiness escaped him,' wrote Ségur. '"Here at last is this famous city.... It is high time."' He was deeply moved: the moment seemed to him the summit of life's achievement. His officers, who had kept their distance since Borodino, crowded round him with congratulations, and the nearest troops shouted, 'Moscou!' Sergeant Bourgogne, one of the few non-commissioned men to leave his memoirs, wrote: 'Many capitals have I seen, such as Paris, Berlin, Warsaw, Vienna and Madrid, but this was quite different; the effect was to me – in fact, to everyone – magical. At that sight, troubles, dangers, fatigues, privations were all forgotten, and the pleasure of entering Moscow absorbed all our minds.'

Napoleon now approached the Dorogomilov Gate, the western entrance on the Smolensk road, and waited there for two hours, expecting a deputation of civic leaders to meet him, if not with keys and gratitude, at least with humility. No such deputation appeared. Only now did he learn that the city was all but abandoned. Eventually, sensing an anticlimax, a member of his staff rounded up a few poor bystanders and pushed them towards him. They said that nearly everyone had left the city, but they would do their best to make his visit a pleasant one. He turned away in contempt. He ordered Murat to enter, while he remained for the night in a tavern in Dorogomilov suburb, being persuaded of the danger of assassination if the city were not occupied ahead of him.

Murat, dressed in his most splendid uniform and a plume-decked Polish cap, advanced cautiously with a cavalry escort to the bridge over the Moskva, found it destroyed, and forded it to approach the Kremlin walls. Here there was a momentary skirmish, with Cossacks, some said, but others mentioned only a few drunken men and women who fired from the battlements. The Kremlin gates, which were barred, were stove in without difficulty, and Murat rode inside to inspect the fortifications and the Imperial Palace. Napoleon followed next morning, 15 September, dressed in his usual dark-green uniform of a colonel in the Chasseurs. He found the streets deserted, but all the larger buildings filled with deserters, the wounded and the poor. The army poured in to occupy the entire city as far as its outer gates, according to previous orders which had allocated the different quarters to the different Corps.

The Kremlin - fortress, barracks, arsenal, palace, and the site of the holiest cathedrals - rises on a prominent hill above a bend in the Moskva, and is ringed by a crenellated brick wall originally built by Italians at the end of the sixteenth century. At intervals it is surmounted by magnificent towers with gateways below them approached by bridges over the moat, like the Trinity Tower by which Napoleon entered. Although he cannot have failed to be impressed by the history, culture and pride which these buildings represented, nor remained totally indifferent to their religious significance, he found the imperial apartments disappointing. They had seldom been used by the Tsar since the capital had been transferred to St Petersburg a century earlier, and it was only on ceremonial occasions, like a wedding, a coronation or an official visit, that he resided there. The palace 'was a miserable dwelling for so powerful a sovereign', wrote Ségur. 'There is not a nobleman in Moscow who is not better housed.'

Situated in the heart of the Kremlin opposite the Cathedral of the Assumption, it was known as the Granovitaya (or 'faceted') Palace, after its rusticated stone facings, and had been designed by an Italian architect in 1487. The building, which still exists, would scarcely look out of place in Florence. Its most famous external feature, since demolished, was the marble Red Staircase, by which the Tsars would make their ceremonial descent on their way to the Cathedral. Inside there were three drawing-rooms, and a great hall, supported by a central pillar and orna-mented with religious paintings, which was used by the Tsars as an audience chamber and banqueting hall. The lesser rooms were sparsely furnished – the state bedroom lacked even curtains or shutters – but the ornaments, a heterogeneous accumulation of porcelain, old armour, an amber toilet-set, the clothes of Peter the Great and the Empress Catherine, candelabra and an old golden throne, were undisturbed. Even the clocks were still tick-ing. Napoleon hung up the Gérard portrait of the King of Rome on a free space between them. Having inspected the whole Kremlin complex, he went to bed early, confessing for once that he was tired.

Once again he had forbidden his men to pillage, and once again his orders were ignored. It was too much to expect of soldiers who had endured such hardships and been promised such a prize. In the palaces they found footmen in livery who did nothing to prevent their entry, and they wandered through the ballrooms and libraries amazed to find in them 'a strange imitation of France', ormolu cabinets and Watteaus on the walls. They helped themselves to clothes and the more portable trea-sures, and feasted on the delicacies and the wine. The officers commandeered princely apartments, and horses were stabled in the churches. Moscow, on this first day, was not 'sacked', and its remaining people were little molested, but greed is conta-gious, and drink its stimulus, and even if it had not been for the fire, which removed all inhibitions, the city would slowly have been stripped of its wealth and the population's worst fears realized. For the moment the soldiers were slightly awed by what they found, and instinctively guarded the city from damage because it was to become, for all they knew, their winter quarters.

It may be that drunken troops, elated and careless, accidentally started some of the fires which Napoleon had noticed as he rode into the city. The criminals and poor, offered an unhoped-for opportunity for looting and orgy, added to the fire risk. Other Russians may soberly have turned to arson as a patriotic gesture. But today, when we can sift all the evidence, there can remain little doubt that the conflagration was started deliberately by Rostopchin's order. He had removed or rendered unusable all the fire-engines, and sunk the fire-floats in the river. He had distributed explosive fuses among reliable saboteurs, who, when caught in the act of firing them, boasted that they were acting under the Governor's orders. A French actress, Louise Fusil, of whom we shall hear more in this narrative, recorded that on the day before the surrender, the police knocked at her door to urge her to fly, 'as the city was going to be set on fire, and the fire-pumps had been taken away'. Men and women were seen running from house to house, throwing in their prepared grenades. There is evidence even more conclusive. The subsequent report of Police-Superintendent Voronenko to the metropolitan authorities stated: 'On 14 September, at five in the morning, Count Rostopchin ordered me to go to the wine-arcade and the customs shed, and in the event of a sudden entry by the enemy troops, to destroy everything by fire, which order I carried out in various places as far as was possible in sight of the enemy until 10 pm.' In a letter to his wife written just before he left the city, Rostopchin declared that he had made every preparation to burn the city, and from a hill just outside it he bade his son take a last look at Moscow: 'In a few hours it will be no more than dust and ashes.'

Rostopchin was acting on his own initiative. Kutuzov had not ordered or approved it: nor the Tsar. Although not a crazed Nero, he was a man of volatile emotions, insisting that Moscow be defended street by street, then urging the people to abandon it; boasting at first that he had stage-managed the fire, later in his Memoirs denying it. It could be seen, as Tolstoy described it in *War and Peace*, as 'the crowning glory of the Russian people', or as an act of unforgivable sacrilege. If the former, it was a patriotic gesture on the grandest scale. It would sully Napoleon's victory, rob him of his prize, of supplies and winter quarters, and force his retreat. It would be the most dramatic proof of Russia's determination to resist to the end. Stendhal wrote, 'Rostopchin will be judged as a rogue or as a Roman. Time will show.' When the news reached London three weeks later, he was hailed as a Roman, the author of one of the most magnificent acts in history, and so Rostopchin intended it, but when the Muscovites returned to find their city in ruins, and rounded on him with reproaches, he claimed that the French had burnt it. The argument did not carry conviction. The French would have had no motive. Yet there remain puzzles about the fire. Why should the poor have contributed to the destruction of their loot? The Kremlin was not sabotaged, though it contained powder and ammunition which would have blown it to pieces, and Napoleon was likely to make his headquarters there. Possibly Rostopchin's nerve failed him. He could not bring himself to destroy the holiest site in Russia.

When Napoleon was woken at 4 am on 16 September, at first he insisted that the fire must be accidental. Even the Russians were incapable of such a sacrifice. It must be the work of criminals and drunks. Then incendiaries in police uniforms were brought to him, with combustible materials in their hands. He ordered their immediate execution, and any others caught red-handed were to be shot on sight or hanged from the trees as a warning. He was told that the fire was by now very serious, and wishing to see it for himself, he climbed to the top of Ivan the Great's Bell Tower, which still dominates the Kremlin. The sight was terrifying. The fire had spread during the night from the bazaar where it had started in earnest to engulf the whole northern and western quarters of the city. His mood wavered between admiration and outrage. 'What a people! They are Scythians. What resoluteness! The barbarians!' A stiff wind from the north was driving the flames towards the centre, the Kremlin. A single spark could detonate the munitions in the Arsenal. The Guard, who were quartered there, were dowsing the beams and stamping out the embers, and Napoleon went to encourage them, till persuaded that he was in danger of his life. The bridge linking the Kremlin to the quays was bursting into flames. The stables and palace roof were catching fire. His adjutants begged him to leave before it was too late. He could not command his army from the middle of a furnace. An incendiary was found within the Kremlin itself. He was bayonetted to death. It was this incident that decided Napoleon to retreat. He left the Kremlin at 5.30 pm.

It is an example of the unreliability of the evidence that even at this memorable moment, accounts of Napoleon's escape by officers who accompanied him vary in significant detail. Ségur says that they left by a postern gate on the riverside.

> Being closer to the fire, we could neither retreat nor remain where we were. The only street [north-east], winding and all in flames, seemed more like an entrance into the inferno than an exit from it. Without hesitating, the Emperor, on foot, dashed into the dangerous passage. He strode forwards through the flames to the crash of collapsing archways, falling rafters and melting iron roofs. The ruins hindered his footsteps. We walked upon burning ground, between two walls of fire. The heat burned our eyes, but we had to keep them open and alert to the danger. The stifling air, the flying sparks and tongues of flame scorched the air we breathed. Our breath drew dry, short, gasping, and we almost choked from the smoke.

Caulaincourt's testimony is less dramatic. He says that instead of walking through the fire, they found horses by the river and rode over the Moskva bridge to take the Mojaisk road by which they had entered, and regained the river a league from the city. All agree that their destination was the Petrovsky Palace, six miles from the Kremlin, which was already guarded by Eugène's troops.

It is a large brick palace, now an Air Force Academy, with a semi-circular courtyard in front of a high-domed building of pseudo-Gothic design, built in 1775–82 as a country house for Catherine the Great. Although it was almost empty of furniture, its setting in a lovely park well clear of the blazing city at last gave Napoleon a taste of imperial luxury. Here he remained three days, issuing orders to quench a fire which was now utterly beyond control.

The wind, heightened by the conflagration and contributing to it, veered from quarter to quarter, as in London in 1666 and Chicago in 1871. It carried sparks and burning embers across the widest streets, and twisted back on itself to engulf in flame the buildings that had hitherto been spared. It was said that the blaze was so great that at night one could read a book by its brilliance six miles off. Some, like Stendhal, found it magnificent. 'Our way', he wrote, 'was lit by the finest blaze in the world, in the form of a huge pyramid, whose base is on the earth and whose spire rises towards heaven.' Four-fifths of Moscow was utterly destroyed, the remaining fifth saved by a sudden change in wind-direction and a deluge of rain. The Kremlin survived almost intact because it stood above the houses like an Acropolis, and the Guard remained there to extinguish any burgeoning blaze. The fire lasted at its height from 15 to 18 September. Some of the larger stone houses escaped, but of others all that remained were chimneys rising like isolated columns over a tangle of charred beams. Most of the churches, on islands in the middle of squares, like the most famous of all, St Basil's Cathedral in the Red Square, were spared, and into them the people crowded for sanctuary.

Discipline in the army, instead of being tightened by the crisis, fell apart. Encouraged to save what they could from the larger buildings, especially food supplies, they looted them. Theft was excused as salvage, 'disputing with the fire their natural prey', as Chambray put it. What property could be considered private when everything would soon be destroyed, and when the Russians themselves were responsible for starting it? The troops outside the city sent in their teams to collect what they regarded as their rightful share. Furs, silks, silver, jewellery and spirits were the main prizes, but fine porcelain was smashed in ignorance of its value. The streets, when not choked with debris, were rendered impassable by abandoned furniture and carriages found too heavy to drag away. There was much drunkenness. As the soldiers were heedless of orders, the rabble joined in. Bands of inebriated soldiers and civilians roamed the streets dressed in rich oriental clothes, aping the Tartars, Cossacks and Chinese. The Poles and Rhinelanders, it was said, were the most undisciplined, and having exhausted, as they thought, the resources of the surviving palaces, they turned on the inhabitants, their partners in crime, stripping them of their loot and any garments that caught their fancy. Any that resisted were clubbed to death. The churches were invaded; priests forced to reveal their treasures. Markets were set up in the squares at which valuables changed hands at absurdly low prices, especially to officers, who felt no shame in bargaining for stolen property with their men, and were more appreciative of its true worth.

Ségur quotes a significant example. He saw a case of rare liqueurs exchanged for a loaf of bread. The army, and still more the civilians, while not short of drink and luxuries like sugar, coffee and preserves, were already deprived of nourishing food. Men were diving into the river to recover the grain which Rostopchin had ordered to be dumped there. The peasants refused to bring in from the surrounding country corn and hay to sell to the army, and foragers sent to collect it ran the risk of being cut off by Cossacks. As Napoleon rode back from the Petrovsky Palace to the Kremlin on 18 September, he saw bivouacked in the streets soldiers stained with mud and blackened by smoke, cooking horseflesh on fires made from precious mahogany furniture and doors, eating these concoctions off silver plate, and reclining afterwards on silk sofas wrapped in Parisian fabrics and rich Siberian furs. 'During our march', wrote Fezensac, 'the thud of our drums, the sound of martial music, added an even sadder note to this spectacle, recalling as it did the idea of a triumph amid a scene of destruction, misery and death.'

Napoleon again ordered the looting to stop in order to conserve whatever supplies remained, and told the citizens that he could not feed them. They must leave the city, and beg or barter for food in the countryside. Gradually the army's discipline was restored, perhaps from shame at their past excesses or fear of punishment, but more likely because there was a growing awareness that their survival depended upon their self-control. Strict rationing was enforced. Hidden stores of food came to light in cellars and walled-up larders. Even pigs and cattle could still sometimes be found in outlying fields, and vegetables in the gardens. Daru, his quartermaster, assured Napoleon that he need not leave Moscow for fear that the army would starve, even if it remained there the whole winter. He was over-optimistic. There was no immediate crisis, but there was certainly not the 'abundance of supplies' that Napoleon had promised in his famous Order of the Day on the eve of Borodino.

On that occasion he had also promised his men 'good winter quarters' and 'a prompt return to our motherland'. The two promises were in a sense contradictory. The Russian winter lasts five months, November till March. Were they to be denied their 'prompt return' for that long? And how would their victory remain permanent if they retreated, leaving Russia unconquered and Moscow to be re-occupied? The dilemma was as evident to the soldiers in their charred billets or in camps outside the city as it was to Napoleon in the Kremlin. His hope was that Alexander would offer peace now that his religious capital was captured and burnt, his army demoralized by the loss of it, and so weakened and dispersed that it was in no fit state to attempt a counter-offensive. In all Napoleon's previous campaigns victory in a major battle followed by the surrender of a capital city had meant the conclusion of hostilities. Now he was prepared to offer terms that seemed to him generous. Alexander need do no more than re-establish their relationship on the conditions agreed at Tilsit, which implied, above all, the reimposition of the blockade against the British.

He misunderstood the Tsar's character and the pressures upon him. Caulaincourt had repeatedly warned him of Alexander's tenacity of purpose, but was disbelieved. If Alexander had been seen to bargain with his nation's enemy, he would have risked his throne, perhaps his life. There was no possibility of compromise. When he was in Moscow in late July, the acclaim of the people and the eagerness of the nobles to pledge their serfs and the merchants their riches for the defence of their country had made it impossible for him, even if he had wished it, to betray their trust. 'I would sooner let my beard grow to the waist and eat potatoes in Siberia,' he had declared. Added to this was his growing conviction that Napoleon was doomed to fail in Russia. The dreadful Russian losses at Borodino, the fall of Moscow and the fire, did nothing to diminish his resolution. Depressed as he was by these disasters, and held by some in St Petersburg to be responsible for them, he saw the hazards of Napoleon's situation even more clearly than Napoleon did himself.

So Napoleon's appeals for peace remained unanswered. There were three of them. One of his difficulties was that he could find no suitable intermediary. In Moscow itself there was no responsible person willing to act for him. The few remaining Russians who had occupied official positions refused even to meet him, giving as their excuse that they had no clothes fit to wear in his presence. Napoleon was obliged to employ the senior of his prisoners, the brother of the Russian Minister in Kassel, to take a letter to St Petersburg. This letter, dated 20 September, began unctuously: 'If your Majesty still conserves for me some remnant of your former feelings, you will take this letter in good part.' He assured the Tsar that the fire had been started by Rostopchin, and that the French had done their best to quench it. He proposed not a capitulation, but a compromise peace. The letter, to which no reply was sent, only reinforced Alexander's belief that Napoleon was in serious trouble.

The second attempt was more dramatic. Napoleon tried to prevail upon Caulaincourt to go to St Petersburg under a flag of truce, since he of all the French was most acceptable to the Tsar. Caulaincourt replied that the mission would be useless. He would not even be received at the Court where he had lately been Ambassador, and from his knowledge of the Tsar, Alexander would never sign a peace so long as Napoleon remained in Moscow. As the offer would certainly be refused, it was better not to make it. It would be taken as additional evidence of the Emperor's embarrassment and anxiety. Napoleon was undaunted. Convinced that Alexander had no confidence in his generals and was nervous that the next hostile step would be an advance on St Petersburg itself, he turned to General Lauriston, who had succeeded Caulaincourt in the Embassy. As it would be difficult for him to pass through the Russian lines without a *laissez passer*, he must first approach Kutuzov through Murat's outposts south of Moscow. Lauriston set off on 4 October. Kutuzov at first refused to see him, then relented, and treated him with feigned courtesy. According to Sir Robert Wilson, who was at Kutuzov's headquarters, Lauriston began by reproaching the Russian commander for the peasants' barbaric treatment of the French foragers. Kutuzov answered that he could not civilize in three months a nation who regarded the enemy as a marauding force of Tartars under a Genghis Khan. When Lauriston protested that the parallel was grossly exaggerated, Kutuzov replied, 'It may be, but not in the eyes of the common people. I can only answer for my troops.' After this frigid start, Lauriston asked in his Emperor's name for an armistice: 'You must not think that we wish it because our affairs are desperate. Our two armies are about equal in strength. It is true that you are nearer your supplies and reinforcements than we are, but we have ours too.' As for the fire, he disclaimed any responsibility. 'It would have been inconsistent with the French character. If we take London, we shall not set fire to it.' Kutuzov replied shortly that he had no authority to conclude an armistice, and he could not allow Lauriston to proceed to St Petersburg. Instead, he would send a member of his own staff, Prince Volkonsky, to deliver Napoleon's letter to the Tsar, and he accompanied it by his recommendation that it should be ignored. Alexander agreed. 'Peace?' he said to Volkonsky. 'But as yet we have not made war. My campaign is only just beginning.'

Napoleon sent Lauriston to Kutuzov once again, on 14 October, this time with a letter from Berthier asking for 'arrangements which will give to the war a character conformable to the established rule of warfare', meaning a non-existent Geneva Convention which might restrain the Russian peasants from their inhuman conduct. Kutuzov replied that 'it is difficult to control a people who for 300 years have never known war within their frontiers, who are ready to immolate themselves for their country, and who are not susceptible to the distinction between what is and what is not the usage of civilized warfare'. After this, Napoleon accepted that peace could not be won by negotiation or appeals for fair play.

Although he conceded that Kutuzov's was a noble letter, he must have been startled by the claim that Russia had not been invaded for three centuries, for at that moment he was reading Voltaire's *History of Charles XII*, and in particular the chapters which describe how the Swedish King's army of 20,000 infantry and 24,000 horse crossed the Dnieper in 1708 and was cut to pieces near Poltava. It had endured such bitter weather that the very birds froze on the wing and fell as if shot. The lesson was lost on Napoleon. For the moment, the climate remained exceptionally mild, 'finer than at Fontainebleau', he exclaimed, refusing to believe Caulaincourt's warning that the Russian winter, when it came, was blistering. His immediate concern, while he waited for Alexander's response, was the problem of communications and supply.

The Moscow army was living in, and off, what remained of the city and its stores. The troops outside it, deployed up to thirty miles east and south, were worse off. The serfs hid their provisions, even when offered money by the French, and as they remained stationary, the army soon exhausted what meagre crops and herds they could seize in the immediate neighbourhood of their camps. As they foraged further afield, they were increasingly exposed to the vengeance of the Cossacks and the people. A French general came under a white flag to complain of their cruelty in falling upon 'poor men only going in search of a little hay', and Murat personally sought out Miloradovich to beg him to allow his troops to forage with impunity. If the request were refused, he would be obliged to escort them with cavalry and artillery. 'This is exactly what I wish,' replied the Russian. Would you want to deprive us of the pleasure of taking your finest cavalry *comme des poules*?' The Cossack patrols were growing so bold that some of them penetrated the suburbs of Moscow itself.

Communications with the major depots at Smolensk and beyond were becoming equally precarious. Most couriers got through, riding alone at full stretch and with fresh horses awaiting them at intervals, and from Paris despatches usually arrived within fifteen days. The slow convoys took their chance between one defended locality and the next. A lieutenant in charge of 105 waggons and 500 reinforcements en route from Smolensk to Moscow decided to split his force into sections, to allow the more mobile vehicles to hurry. Gradually the entire convoy melted away, ambushed by partisans as they left the road to forage. Under such leaders as Denis Davidov, Chetvertakov and Figner, the peasants began to organize into semi-disciplined bands. Davidov's instructions were merciless. Receive the enemy with bows, he told them, offer them food and drink, and when they are drunk and asleep, slit their throats. Then bury their bodies in the forest or pigsties, and scatter twigs over the new-turned earth, for if the graves are discovered, you will all be killed. The toll of French and allied casualties became so serious that Napoleon ordered that no force weaker than 1,500 men should take the Smolensk road. Every day, wrote an observer in the Russian headquarters, prisoners in parties of 50, even 100, were brought in by the Cossacks. In five days, 1,342 were delivered to Kutuzov, most of them wounded. 'Of course,' he went on, 'many more were killed, for such is the inveterate hatred of the peasants that they will buy prisoners off the Cossacks and put them to death.' This grisly alliance between the loose-reined horsemen and the enraged serfs was something that Napoleon had never previously encountered, even in Spain. It added greatly to his sense of isolation, and to his dawning realization of the strength and unity of Russian resistance.

His mood was unpredictable and febrile, and the reasons were clear. His triumph had been short-lived, and he was uncertain how to act next. He found occupation for the Moscow soldiers in daily parades, in the fortification of outlying monasteries as a defensive ring around the city, and in making half-hearted preparations for the winter, like constructing sledges, lining coats with fur collars and manufacturing simple gauntlets. But his hesitation and growing impotence were revealed in his issue of impossible orders. Told that he was desperately short of horses, he replied that 20,000 must be bought locally, when not a single one was to be found. Told that supplies of fodder were running low, he ordered more to be collected, but from where? The whole army was to be reclothed and shod, but there were only the inadequate materials saved from the fire. Alternately he was sullen and intensely active. Ségur wrote, 'He prolonged his meals, which had hitherto been simple and short. He seemed anxious to stifle thought by repletion. He would pass whole hours half-reclined, as if torpid, with a novel in his hands.' In a pathetic attempt to simulate normality and even gaiety in a scene of such desolation and foreboding, he organized entertainments, and himself attended a performance of the comedy *Guerre Ouverte* in the private theatre of a surviving palace (the wooden Grand Théâtre having been totally destroyed by the fire), where he heard the French actress Louise Fusil sing sentimental songs, like the lament of a chevalier on leaving his betrothed:

Bientôt vainqueur, je reviendrai vers toi.
Et j'obtiendrai le prix de ma vaillance.
Mon cœur sera le gage de ta foi
Et mon amour celui de ta constance.

The band of the Old Guard played the accompaniment. Napoleon demanded an encore. Fusil's voice, which had never been anything very remarkable, trembled with apprehension.

Napoleon now bent his mind seriously to the future. On 30 September he called his inner council to the Kremlin – Murat, Davout, Eugène and Berthier – and raised with them the possibility of marching immediately on St Petersburg, where Macdonald would join him. Ségur said that he was very much excited, his eyes shining. The Marshals were astonished by the proposal, and began to state all the objections to it. St Petersburg was 350 miles away. It would take the Grand Army at least six weeks to reach it, the later part of the march coinciding with the onset of extreme cold. The army was in no fit state to march, even in fine weather. It would find no supplies on the sterile road. They would be leaving behind them a Russian army which was rapidly regaining its strength and would have little difficulty in re-occupying Moscow. Napoleon reproached them for not understanding the grandeur of his plan. His army needed the stimulus of a new chapter to the campaign, to 'distract it from its losses by persuading it that that it was still fit for any undertaking' (Caulaincourt). The revival of Russian morale was much exaggerated. Their generals, even Kutuzov, longed for peace. Murat supported this erroneous opinion, misled and flattered by the compliments paid to him on his occasional parleys with the enemy. In the end Napoleon gave way. It is doubtful whether his St Petersburg project was anything more than a sudden fantasy to console himself for the predicament he had created. If both capitals could be occupied, the chances of peace would obviously be greater, as Hitler thought too. But the difficulties and risks would be too great, as he admitted at St Helena.

What options remained? He could advance eastwards into central Russia, but what would that achieve? He could stay in Moscow all winter, and attack St Petersburg in the spring. He could retreat to Smolensk and Vitebsk, where he would be nearer his bases, and start the campaign afresh in 1813, this time making a major thrust towards St Petersburg from Riga. He could seek a second major battle with Kutuzov south of Moscow, and if successful, continue into the warmer, more fruitful and unravished regions of southern Russia round Kiev. Or he could abandon the whole campaign.

The most tempting of these plans, to which he clung for several weeks, was to winter in Moscow and restore his strength. But there were two drawbacks to it. First, he would be absent from Paris for at least six months more. While his dictated orders were incessant, and few of them failed to reach their destinations, it was impossible to rule a vast Empire from its extreme boundary. His hold on Paris itself could not be taken for granted. 'If I'd only been the commander of the army,' he said to Louis Molé in February 1813, 'I'd have stayed in Moscow for the winter. I could have supplied myself. But as Emperor I could not risk the cutting of my communications. France would have been without news of me for six months, and what would happen there during that time?' Secondly, it was by no means certain that he could have supplied himself. He was already perilously over-reached and over-exposed. The supply problem would get worse. His communications could at any moment be cut by Kutuzov if he reoccupied Mojaisk, even Smolensk, for the Russian army was poised on his lightly defended flank. As the Russians grew stronger, he would grow weaker. There were medical problems in the stinking city. He described it in his 26th Bulletin to Paris as 'an impure cess-pool'. Reinforcements were reaching Moscow only in driblets, but from the Ukraine, the Don, they were pouring into the Russian camp, and at Kaluga and Tula Kutuzov had depots and factories which would replace all the supplies and munitions he had lost. Napoleon had no accessible equivalents. But if he abandoned Moscow, retreated as far as Smolensk, the world would take it as an admission of failure, 'the watershed of his fame and success' (Thiers), the one conclusion of the campaign which his prestige could not afford.

But say that he held Moscow with a light rearguard, and took his main army south to challenge the Russians to another major battle? When he had defeated them once more, there could be peace, and if there were not, the road to Kiev would be open to him, a road which led to better supplies, and would give him a strategic position strong enough to allow him to return temporarily to Paris. He would have saved his conquest and his reputation. The next year would be decisive. If it were a drawn battle, or Kutuzov evaded him, he could still withdraw to Smolensk without too much loss of dignity, claiming that his short retreat was merely a device to gain a more advantageous position for 1813.

While he was still pondering the alternatives of staying in Moscow or 'advancing south' to cover and excuse what would be in effect a retreat, he tried them out, as so often, on Caulaincourt, knowing that he would receive honest if unwelcome advice. Caulaincourt warned him that he was in a position of great danger. The present stalemate, this 'tacit armistice', was a Russian ruse to lull him into a false sense of security. In St Petersburg they well understood his difficulties. 'What difficulties?' Napoleon asked. 'The winter, Sire, is a big difficulty, to begin with. The lack of stores, of horses for your artillery, of transport for your sick and wounded, the poor clothing for your soldiers. Every man must have a sheepskin, stout fur-lined gloves, a cap with ear-flaps, warm boot-socks, heavy boots to keep his feet from getting frost-bitten. You lack all this. Not a single frost-nail has been forged for the horses' hooves; how are they going to draw the guns? Then there are your communications; the weather is still fine; but what will it be in a month, in a fortnight perhaps, or even less?' These difficulties would exist whether they remained in Moscow or not, but Napoleon, ignoring the ambiguity, replied that the climatic conditions were much exaggerated. In any case the French were 'more robust' than the enemy. The Polish Cossacks whom he expected to join him soon (they never did) would be a match for the Russian. He was thinking of holding Moscow with a garrison while he captured Kaluga and made closer contact with his troops on the Dvina. Clearly he was pretending to his generals, even if he did not deceive himself, that all things were simultaneously possible. In the event, none of them was.

It is one of the most interesting situations in military history. Here was Napoleon at the summit of his career, if not at the height of his intellectual power, and at the furthest geographical limit of his conquests, faced by the choice between risking all he had gained or humiliating himself and his army by a retreat which might end in equal disaster. Here was Kutuzov, defeated at Borodino (as he must by this time have privately acknowledged), but with his army intact, growing stronger and in a position to threaten Napoleon whether he retreated or not. A younger, bolder man than Kutuzov would have taken the offensive, besieged Moscow and cut the Smolensk road in force. Either commander could remain static: either could make a quick move before winter descended. Of the two, Napoleon was the more impelled to make the first move. If he did not, Kutuzov would have the initiative. Napoleon's famous statement that 'Moscow is not a military position; it is a political position' meant that in the last resort he must give strategy precedence temporarily over politics, and leave the city. He must save the army in such a way that he could claim that his political strength was undiminished. There was only one way to do this. To attack Kutuzov, defeat him, and take the Grand Army into winter quarters further west. Moscow must be yielded to Russia, but at a greater cost to them than to himself. To defeat Kutuzov was an 'indispensable preliminary' (Caulaincourt) to a withdrawal, in order to save face, protect his retreat from continuous harassment, prevent a link-up between Kutuzov and Wittgenstein, and re-open peace talks with the Tsar from a position of reasonable strength. His marshals agreed that this was the only course. It would have been a feasible plan – had it been executed a month earlier. That was Napoleon's own conclusion when he looked back on the campaign from St Helena. 'After arriving in Moscow,' he said, 'I should have crushed what remained of Kutuzov's army, marched on Maloyaroslavets, Tula and Kaluga, then proposed to the Russians to retire without destroying anything.' But still it does not make sense. What would such a retirement have meant compared to total victory?

He seems to have reached a firm decision no sooner than 17 October, when his third approach to the Tsar went unanswered except for Alexander's instruction to Kutuzov to accept no

further parleys. Then Napoleon acted rapidly. The retreat was
to start three days later, and on 18 October he held in the Kremlin courtyard a grand parade of Ney's corps, which had been
spruced up to reassure him that the army was still capable of
anything. During the parade he heard that Murat's advance
guard had been surprised at Vinkovo and escaped with difficulty.
This confirmed his resolution. He would advance his movements
by a day, and leave Moscow on the 19th. 'March to Kaluga!' he
cried, 'and woe betide anyone who obstructs my passage!'

When the French had entered Moscow five weeks earlier, the
Russian army had withdrawn south-east along the Kolomna
road, but, stung by reproaches that he had failed in his duty,
Kutuzov moved it two days later through Podolsk, and then
across country by night, his march illuminated by the Moscow
fire, to cover the roads leading south and south-east to Tula and
Kaluga (see map page 114). This was a stronger position. The
towns were his major depots, and he would be better placed to
threaten Napoleon and recapture Moscow if he should decide to
advance on St Petersburg. The ingenuity of the Fili decision was
now apparent. St Petersburg could be better protected by
stationing the Russian army south of Moscow instead of across
the main Moscow-St Petersburg road.

Murat had pursued the Russians east and south-east, towards
Vladimir and Kolomna, then lost touch with them when Kutuzov switched south. Reproached by Napoleon for his negligence,
Murat offered the curious excuse that he had not wished to harry
the Cossacks when they were on the point of deserting. He did
not regain contact with them till 26 September, some twenty-
five miles south of Moscow. Kutuzov then withdrew to Tarutino, and Murat moved to Vinkovo. The two advance guards
remained for three weeks only an hour's march apart. There
were frequent communications between them, from the Russian
side mainly for the purpose of lulling Napoleon into that 'false
sense of security' of which Caulaincourt had warned him. They
directed their blandishments mainly at Murat himself, assuring
him that never would a Russian shoot at him personally, so
greatly did they esteem his character and courage. When he was
fired on by a Cossack (who missed, and 'had evidently been
imperfectly coached in this new system of advance-guard poli-

tics', as Caulaincourt said with justifiable cynicism), an officer immediately rode up to apologize and promise that the soldier would be punished. Other incidents were less reassuring. When the French occupied Vinkovo, they found Rostopchin's country house in ruins, with a note left for them in his own hand: 'I voluntarily set this house on fire, that it may not be polluted by your presence.'

Kutuzov was under constant pressure to be more aggressive. It was all very well for him to boast, as he did to the Tsar on 12 October, that 'the enemy's graves are already being dug for them in the soil of the Empire'. Graves could not be dug, nor filled, by inaction. His own Chief-of-Staff, Bennigsen, could hardly contain his impatience. Kutuzov now had 100,000 infantry, 20,000 Cossacks and over 600 guns, apart from the swelling bands of partisans. Napoleon had a vast triangle to defend, its tip at Moscow and its broad base 550 miles away on the Niemen. Kutuzov should cut off the tip, entreated Bennigsen. Sir Robert Wilson, still attached to the headquarters, urged him to advance at least as far as Borovsk to threaten the Smolensk road. 'I shall play for time,' was Kutuzov's answer, 'lull Napoleon as much as possible and not disturb him in Moscow. Every device which contributes to this object is preferable to the pursuit of glory.' In other words, *Si vis bellum, para pacem.*

Nevertheless, he decided that a limited attack might allay criticism. He took advantage of an unofficial truce while the French were foraging, and attacked Sebastiani's cavalry Corps at Vinkovo at dawn on 18 October, in the mist. At first the French thought it merely another Cossack patrol, but when the mist lifted, they saw the Russians advancing en masse. The guns opened up on both sides, and the French cavalry charged, only to find themselves heavily outnumbered. Their infantry were forced to withdraw from threatened encirclement in a ravine, leaving behind them thirty cannon and 2,500 casualties. Murat came up with enough troops to hold a position at Voronovo twelve miles in the rear, and Kutuzov, who had never intended the affair to be more than a skirmish to appease his subordinates and frighten Napoleon, refused to send up the reinforcements which Bennigsen demanded. The Russians contented themselves with occupying the French camp at Vinkovo. The battle, which lasted all day, infuriated Napoleon, who blamed Murat for lowering his guard, while admitting that he had retrieved it with great gallantry. He determined to march from Moscow at once to wipe out the dishonour and set his great plan in motion.

CHAPTER SIX

BEGINNING OF THE RETREAT

The march (it could not yet be called a withdrawal, and 'retreat' was unmentionable) began before dawn on 19 October 1812, thirty-five days after the French had entered Moscow. The army now consisted in 87,500 infantry, 14,750 cavalry and 533 guns (Caulaincourt's figures), with a train of some 40,000 carriages and waggons. Behind them came a tail of camp-followers, including French women and children escaping Muscovite revenge, some Russian girls in voluntary captivity, and servants acquired during the city's occupation. 'It looked like a caravan, a wandering nation,' said Ségur, 'or rather, one of those armies of antiquity returning with slaves and spoil after a great devastation.' Every cart and carriage contained loot to bring back to France, much of it hidden under provisions and ammunition. Napoleon had issued orders that needless vehicles must be left behind, and burnt one of his own as an example, but it proved impossible to veto the removal of booty when it was the only compensation and proof of victory he could offer his men, and he himself had taken much of the Kremlin's treasure, including the great cross surmounting the Bell Tower of Ivan the Great, which he intended to erect over the Invalides. Some equipages were luxurious. Louise Fusil had been given a carriage and five horses by a staff-officer, and, wrapped in furs and attended by servants, she drove between the still-smoking ruins to join the procession.

The result was a slow and cumbersome convoy of enormous length (*impedimenta* in its literal sense), in place of a light, mobile force which could strike with the speed of a cobra, as Napoleon had intended. In theory the column carried enough food for twenty days, but there was horse-fodder for less than a week. Mortier was left in Moscow with part of the Young Guard to give the impression that Napoleon's return was probable, but with secret orders to stay there only four days and then leave for Mojaisk, having blown up the Kremlin and other important buildings. Some of the sick and wounded were sent towards Smolensk by the direct road, but many thousands were left in Moscow. Their fate was terrible. In the officers' ward of the Foundling Hospital, for instance, forty out of forty-five died of typhus. When the Young Guard left the city, all surviving casualties were murdered and their corpses thrown into the river.

Not even senior regimental officers knew their destination. Napoleon had never thought it necessary to raise morale by explaining his intentions, but the troops guessed, 'with that intelligence and instinct which characterizes French soldiers' (Fezensac), that they were headed for Kaluga and the warmer country south, and would certainly have to overcome the Russian army which barred their way. In fact, the forthcoming battle was to be followed only by the occupation of Kaluga and possibly Tula, and then the army would march across unravished country to join the old road at Smolensk. There would be no time, with winter approaching, for the longer march through the Ukraine, and the army's reserves lay west, not south. Even this modified plan was later truncated.

They marched in wide parallel columns towards Kaluga, the transports and artillery on the road itself, the infantry and cavalry across the fields on either side, covering about ten miles a day. They did not know when or where they would meet the Russians, as no prisoners were captured, the peasants were dumb with hatred, and no spies had managed to penetrate the enemy lines. Russian intelligence was equally bad. It was not till 22 October that Kutuzov learnt that Napoleon had left Moscow, and for a time he believed that the French were taking the 'old' Kaluga road instead of the new road by Borovsk, and that a second battle of Vinkovo would soon take place. To by-pass him, Napoleon had switched across country at Troitskoe from the old road to the new, and when Kutuzov became aware of it, Napoleon was approaching Borovsk. Even now, the Russians scarcely suspected their danger. A sizeable force under Docturov moved to discover what was happening, and found, instead of the strong patrols they expected, the entire Grand Army, with Napoleon himself in command. The race was now on, between the French to seize, and the Russians to hold, the key point on the new road, a town called Maloyaroslavets. It lies on the south bank of the River Lutza, which was bridged at that point in a ravine, leaving a narrow ledge between the bridge and the wooded escarpment that rises steeply to the town. A church and a few houses stood on this ledge beside the bridge. South of the town the approaches were flatter. Clearly it was an ideal defensive position, as both sides also found in 1941, when it was the site of two major battles, the Germans to capture it and the Russians to retake it a month later.

By an all-night march, 23/24 October, Docturov managed to take the town, driving out a handful of Eugène's advance guard which had occupied part of it, but left the bridge and neighbouring buildings in French hands. The fight for the bridge became intense, each side knowing that the other's main army was approaching and that the position would be far stronger for the Russians if the bridge were destroyed. The French held on, and by 10 am on the 24th their divisions were beginning to cross in strength. Sir Robert Wilson took personal command of a Russian battery and directed its fire on the massed troops as they descended the north bank of the ravine. This imposed a temporary delay, but Delzons's division threw over a second bridge, swarmed across the river and began to scale the escarpment to the town itself. On reaching the crest, they hesitated, and Delzons, taking the lead, was killed, falling into the arms of his brother, who, trying to shield him with his body, was himself hit, and both died together. The town was captured, then lost again, as fresh battalions became engaged on each side. Caulaincourt says that it changed hands seven times during the day. Its wooden houses were in flames, its panicking population of some 10,000 caught between two fires. Raevski came up to Docturov's support, and Eugène threw in his last reserves, the division from north Italy under General Pino. This was decisive. It was the Italians' finest hour (they had arrived too late for Borodino).

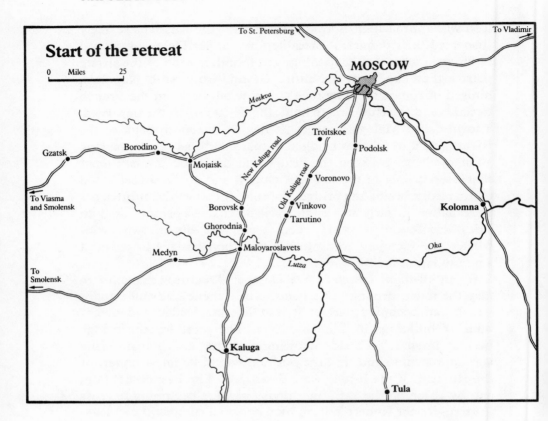

Start of the retreat

0   Miles   25

To St. Petersburg

To Vladimir

MOSCOW

Moskva

Troitskoe

Podolsk

Gzatsk

Borodino

Mojaisk

New Kaluga road

Old Kaluga road

Voronovo

To Viasma
and Smolensk

Borovsk

Vinkovo

Kolomna

Ghorodnia

Tarutino

Medyn

Maloyaroslavets

Oka

Lutza

To
Smolensk

Kaluga

Tula

They retook the town and remained in possession of it till nightfall. For unblooded recruits the achievement was remarkable,
'ignoring the danger', as Ségur said, 'for life is less dear to youth
than to the aged'.

Both commanders-in-chief had been dilatory. Napoleon, who
did not even realize till mid-morning that a battle was in progress, failed to hasten forward his reserves. Kutuzov was so slow
in moving up his main body to Docturov's aid that Sir Robert
Wilson, who had been in the thick of the battle and so more
liable to find fault with those who weren't, accused him of 'sloth,
indecision, panic operations, and a desire to let the enemy pass
unmolested.... He affords a memorable instance of incapacity

in a chief, of an absence of any quality that ought to distinguish a commander.'

The situation now resembled the closing phase of Borodino. Casualties at Maloyaroslavets had been on a much smaller scale (the Russians lost about 7,000, the French and allies 4,000), but, as in the earlier battle, the main positions were in Napoleon's hands and the Russians had fallen back unbroken about a mile behind. It could have been an occasion for a major encounter on the following day, since both armies now faced each other in total strength. Instead, both withdrew.

Napoleon spent the night in a squalid weaver's hut at Ghorodnia, two miles north of the river, his only privacy a blanket dividing the single room into two. There he was joined by Bessières, commanding the cavalry of the Guard, who told him that he had reconnoitred the new Russian position and found it too strong to attack, as it was covered by impassable swamps. Napoleon was utterly depressed, speaking of his waning star: 'I beat them every time,' he said, 'but cannot reach the end.' Unable to sleep, he rode out at 4 am on 25 October with a string of officers but without his usual cavalry escort. Suddenly a throng of Cossacks appeared from nowhere, and had it not been for the warning given by their war-cries, he might not have escaped. Behind this group were a thousand more Cossacks led by Platov, who had crossed the river upstream, captured a few guns and found a gap between the front-line troops and Napoleon's headquarters. It was an inexcusable failure on the part of the Guard to have stationed no pickets and sent out no patrols. Napoleon, with Caulaincourt, Rapp and Bessières, found themselves alone. They drew their swords. The nearest Russian, says Ségur, 'had only to stretch out a hand to seize the Emperor'. Napoleon displayed great coolness. When Rapp snatched the bridle of his horse to take him out of danger, he insisted on standing his ground. Just in time, a squadron of chasseurs came up to fight off the Cossacks, who retired insolently and at walking pace, reloading their muskets, knowing that the speed of their light horses would soon outstrip the French if they came in pursuit. It is not certain that they even realized how great a prize they had missed, for it was still dark.

Napoleon, undismayed by the incident, rode smiling across

the bridge and into Maloyaroslavets. The dreadful scene of carnage in the streets did not upset him, but when he saw that the Russians had abandoned their new positions, his determination failed. He stared ahead for a long time in silence, then rode back to Ghorodnia, where he summoned his Council to a conference. Some historians have called it the most fateful of his career. In the same mean weaver's hut where he had tried to sleep, he invited the advice of Murat, Eugène, Davout, Bessières and Berthier. Nobody even proposed a return to Moscow. All agreed that their destination, and probably their winter quarters, must be Smolensk. Should they march by Kaluga, Medyn or Mojaisk? Murat, full of fire, was for Kaluga, even if that meant, as it probably would, another battle. If they were to retreat, it should be by Mojaisk to join the Smolensk road as soon as possible: the more southerly route by Medyn would mean a flank march under incessant attack, and over unknown country which contained no prepared positions or supplies. Davout favoured the Medyn road to Viasma, as it was shorter, with unburnt villages and perhaps stores of grain. The Mojaisk route would be depressing – nothing but corpses, wounded and famine.

It is significant that none of the generals, except Murat, argued for a renewal of the battle on the Kaluga road, and Murat did not press it strongly. They all recognized the weakness of the Grand Army. Even if they won another battle, they would have great losses, and be encumbered by a mass of wounded who could not be abandoned without dismaying the survivors. They could not risk their remaining horses, which must be kept for hauling the guns and transport. The nights were growing longer and colder; it was no time of year for elaborate manoeuvres. Napoleon listened quietly, let fall a few phrases about the necessity to gain Kaluga and salvage their reputations, but then succumbed to the majority view. He agreed that it was too late for audacity and glory; it was now a question of saving the army. Bessières dared to use for the first time the dread word retreat. It passed unchallenged. Only the route remained undecided, and Napoleon declared for Borovsk–Mojaisk–Gzatsk–Viasma–Smolensk, to escape Kutuzov as far and as soon as possible, at the very moment when Kutuzov himself was retreating south. The two armies turned their backs on each other. Kutuzov, too, for a different reason, wished to avoid another battle. He could defeat Napoleon without one. If necessary, he would even withdraw from Kaluga, south of the Oka. He would build 'a golden road', he said, on which the Emperor would destroy himself.

Napoleon's decision to abandon the Kaluga road, says Eugen Stschepkin in *The Cambridge Modern History*, 'was a course which meant nothing short of destruction for his army', and this has been the general verdict. It requires some examination. Undoubtedly Napoleon was feeling the strain of the long campaign. His willingness to abandon first the St Petersburg plan, and now his Kaluga plan, when his generals objected, indicates, not a greater willingness to listen to advice, but a failure to think out all the consequences before he asked for it. The harlequinade of his army's march from Moscow, its load of useless baggage and mass of camp-followers, show a relaxation of his control and of his troops' self-discipline which at such a critical moment was inexcusable. The young Bonaparte would have seen long in advance the importance of Maloyaroslavets, and advanced much faster towards it and in greater strength. Even if it is granted that the decision to leave Moscow was the correct one, it should never have been undertaken without proper preparation for the winter ahead, which would only have been possible if a much more determined effort had been made to bring up supplies during the thirty-five days that he remained there. As his purpose in moving south from Moscow was to seek out Kutuzov and beat him, why did he shirk the challenge when it came? The arguments raised against the plan at the Ghorodnia conference were the same as those that could have been foreseen before leaving Moscow – fear of further casualties among troops and horses, lack of supplies, shortage of time before the good weather ended.

All that the Maloyaroslavets 'victory' had achieved, if it were not to be followed up, was the waste of ten days and several thousand casualties. Although proportionately Napoleon had suffered in the battle less than Kutuzov, he was left weaker. He had brought upon himself the need to convert a moderately successful advance south into a precipitate retreat north and west. The reasons for the failure of the campaign lay further back, perhaps even as far back as the decision to embark upon it at all.

To withdraw from the Kaluga road was a consequence of poor strategic planning, not the cause of his ultimate undoing. Whether he withdrew north-west to Mojaisk, or west through Medyn, was of minor importance. When he made the decision he did not even know that Kutuzov had left the latter road uncovered. The circuitous route which he did choose added only two days' march to the fifty (Moscow–Vilna) of the retreat, and there were some advantages in the northern road. Junot's Corps was already at Mojaisk, and Mortier was approaching it. In spite of the slightly longer march, Napoleon managed to outstrip his pursuers until the Beresina, but he did not, and could not, outstrip the winter. Whichever route he had taken after Maloyaroslavets, the army would still have been destroyed. To imagine that at Kaluga and beyond he would have swum into a region of peace, warmth and plenty, is wishful thinking, of which those harassed men at Ghorodnia were innocent. They took the decision, not in panic, but with calm deliberation.

Mortier remained in Moscow with 8,000 men of the Young Guard until 23 October, pulling them back into the Kremlin to escape the encroaching Cossacks and the reviving animosity of the people. For four days he was virtually besieged. He carried out Napoleon's orders 'to blow up the Kremlin' with scant efficiency. A heavy downpour of rain and the prompt arrival of Russian troops prevented the majority of the planned explosions. Three towers, a stretch of the wall and a part of the Arsenal were destroyed, and of Ivan's great bell tower, which Napoleon had wished to see toppled from its dominating position, only an annex was blown up. The tons of explosive placed in the palace cellars failed to detonate. With great difficulty the French escaped from the citadel, having lit their fuses, and made their way westwards out of the city. The explosion, partial though it was, could be heard from thirty miles away.

The main army retreated in low spirits from Maloyaroslavets to Mojaisk. The distance was about fifty miles on a poor road, but they covered it in two days, hastened by Napoleon's insistence that they make the most of the still fine weather. The next day, 29 October, they marched through Borodino. The highway skirted the main battlefield, and many averted their eyes, but the stench of unburied corpses and the wheeling carrion crows were inescapable reminders of what they had suffered there only seven weeks before. Around the battered redoubts ('like extinct volcanoes', said Ségur) still lay the debris of the battle – helmets, weapons, broken drums, bloodstained standards. The wolves had made a meal of 30,000 corpses. It was said, incredibly, that there was one man still alive, a soldier with both legs broken who had taken refuge inside a dead horse and lived off putrefying flesh and stagnant water, and that his life was saved. No halt was made to survey this graveyard of men so uselessly sacrificed, and the army filed past in silence. Napoleon gave it scarcely a glance. At the Kolotskoye monastery, the main French hospital, such pretended indifference was impossible. A handful of surgeons had managed to keep alive a few hundred wounded, who dragged themselves forward to implore the army to take them home. Some were found places on carts to join the wounded from Maloyaroslavets, but hardly one reached France. The others were abandoned to certain death. That same night, at Gzatsk, the army felt the first touch of frost.

Napoleon sent for Caulaincourt, in whom he was placing increasing trust as the only man of his suite who thoroughly understood the Russian character. It was 2 am. The Emperor was in bed. He told the Master of the Horse to speak frankly about their prospects. Caulaincourt needed no pressing, but how could he give the Emperor any consolation? He described what would be the inevitable outcome of the army's slow disintegration and the worsening weather. He recalled the Tsar's ominous reply to Napoleon's latest offer of peace, 'My campaign is just beginning,' and insisted that this warning must be taken literally. 'The further the season advanced, the more everything would favour the Russians, and, above all, the Cossacks.' Napoleon seemed unconvinced. The superior intelligence of the French would prevail. Their power of initiative would protect them against the cold. He spoke of winter quarters, not now at Smolensk, but at Orsha or Vitebsk. Within a few days, he deluded himself, he would be joined by the Polish Cossacks, who would entirely change the situation. The Russians were suffering too, and Kutuzov did not want a battle. At Smolensk they would find supplies and reinforcements, and again on the Dvina. From Vilna warm clothing would be sent forward. They would be strong enough to pass a quiet winter even if the Russian army from the Danube linked up with Kutuzov's. He might even be spared time enough to return to Paris. Caulaincourt, in despair at such optimism, was able to approve strongly of this last suggestion. Napoleon must command from the Tuileries, he said, as news of his retreat would create consternation. He ended by repeating his warning: there was worse to come. Napoleon knew it, but insisted that he had escaped from tighter spots before.

The army was now stumbling along the single road, the column strung out by delays and stragglers to a length of fifty miles. It was exposed not only to stabbing attacks on each flank by Cossack raiders, but to the constant threat that Kutuzov would manage to push ahead of them with a large force and block their further progress, or cut off, one by one, like a string of sausages, the divisions which formed the rearguard and the centre.

Kutuzov, however, had no intention of striking a major blow against Napoleon, at least until he was able to concentrate against him the two other armies, Wittgenstein's in the north and Chichagov's in the south, to join with his own to squeeze him out of Russia. Kutuzov's strategy, and the personality which inspired it, are hard to unravel, for he did not choose to explain it to his staff, and died early in the following year before putting his recollections on paper. By Tolstoy he was regarded as the greatest hero of the campaign, wise, subtle and noble, and under Tolstoy's influence he still is today. At the time he was lampooned as indecisive and inept, by some even as imbecile and a traitor, accused not only of allowing Napoleon's escape, but wanting it. It was said, largely on the evidence of a chance remark reported by Sir Robert Wilson, that his purpose was no more than to expel Napoleon from Russia, not to destroy him, for England, an untrustworthy ally, would be the only ultimate beneficiary of his death or capture. Revenge should be confined to mutilating, not annihilating, Napoleon. If he crossed Russia's borders with a remnant of his army, and raised a new one in France, that was no concern of Russia, which would have demonstrated his fallibility and need fear him no longer. It was, if this version of his thoughts is correct, the motive of a great patriot, an isolationist. But is it correct?

After the battle of Maloyaroslavets, and on receiving news of Napoleon's retreat, Kutuzov issued the following proclamation to his troops:

At the moment when the enemy entered Moscow, all the wild hopes he entertained vanished before his eyes. There he expected plenty and security; there he was bereft of all the necessities of life. Worn with long and incessant marching, exhausted through lack of food, harassed by our raiding parties who cut off the few supplies that were coming to him, he lost thousands of his soldiers, who fell to the swords of irregulars and in no honourable fight.

No prospect faced him but the vengeance of a nation that has sworn to destroy his army. Every Russian showed him a hero in whom his false promises had bred both contempt and horror, indeed every rank of citizen in the Empire has united to present an unsurpassable barrier to his efforts. After incurring losses beyond counting, he has seen at last, but too late, the folly of his hope that the foundations of the Empire could be shaken by the taking of Moscow. There remained no safety for him except in hasty flight. He therefore evacuated Moscow on the 23rd of this month, abandoning his wounded to the vengeance of an angry people.

The hideous excesses of which he was guilty in the capital are already sufficiently known, and have stamped every Russian heart with a strong will for vengeance. In the very moment of his going he showed his baffled anger by the destruction of the Kremlin. There the divine power intervened for us, and saved the cathedral and our holy shrines.

We must hasten in pursuit of this sacrilegious enemy, while other armies, in Lithuania [Wittgenstein], work with us for his destruction. Already he is in headlong flight. He is burning his waggons, abandoning his baggage and the treasures his impious hands have snatched from the very altars of the Lord. Desertion and famine spread confusion around him. The murmuring of his soldiers rises behind him like the mutter of threatening waves.

While this hideous clamour escorts the French retreat, in the ears of the Russians there rings the spirited voice of their

Monarch. Soldiers, hear the words he speaks to us: 'Quench the flames of Moscow with the enemy's blood.' Russians, obey that solemn order. Then your country, satisfied with this just revenge, will retire content from the field of war, and, behind its vast frontiers, take up its noble stance between Peace and Glory.

Soldiers of Russia, God is your guide.

Several points in this remarkable document demand attention. Addressed to his soldiers, it was couched in such elevated language that it could barely have been comprehensible to any except the officers, but there is an undercurrent of religious fervour well attuned to the national character. Napoleon's name is never mentioned, not even by insult. Nothing is said about Borodino or Maloyaroslavets. The burning of Moscow is not attributed to the French. Their deprivations and brutality while they remained there are much exaggerated. There is no direct appeal to the serfs to rise against them or burn the villages. Indeed, the losses of the French at the hands of the partisans are described as dishonourable. While the word 'destruction' is used, it is qualified by the phrase, 'Your country, satisfied with this just revenge, will retire content from the field of war, and, behind its vast frontiers, take up its noble stance.' There is no indication of the method by which Napoleon would be defeated, and if this was because the proclamation might fall into enemy hands (indeed, Napoleon received a copy of it in Smolensk), it is significant that Kutuzov's emphasis was not on crushing him but on expelling him; on the appeal to God, not arms.

He was under the ultimate direction of the Tsar and the more immediate pressures exerted by his generals. Alexander played little direct part at this stage of the campaign, studying the reports which reached him and turning in hours of crisis to the Scriptures. His general advice was that Wittgenstein and Chichagov should converge from each side to block Napoleon's retreat while Kutuzov attacked him from behind. It was the obvious triangular strategy, created by the pattern of Napoleon's advance in a deep arrow-head. But events need not wait upon the convergence of the three armies. Napoleon was already in so desperate a situation, and confined to a single road, that Kutuzov alone could break his army apart. Kutuzov saw it differently. There was no need to expend Russian lives to oust Napoleon from Russia. He need only shadow his southern flank, waste his army by probes, cut off its extremities when possible, and allow the winter, starvation and the psychological effects of retreat to do the rest. The threat of major action was as effective as its execution.

So Kutuzov's movements were slow and circuitous. He followed parallel to Napoleon with his main army on the Medyn–Smolensk road, and permitted only lunges against him. If Napoleon regained Smolensk, that was no disadvantage, as he would soon have to leave it again. Gradually Russia would be liberated without a battle. That was his hope and intention. In *War and Peace* Tolstoy puts into his mind the reflection: 'Patience and time are my two valiant allies! The apple is better not picked while it is still green. It will fall of itself when ripe.' And of his critics: 'They would like to run and look at the damage they have done. Wait a bit and you'll see. This everlasting talk of manoeuvres, of attacks! What for? Only to gain distinction for themselves! As if fighting were some jolly exercise!'

Looking back on the campaign from the security of 1813, this was a strategy that seemed bound to succeed, because it did succeed. But there was an alternative that might have succeeded even better: to destroy Napoleon before he reached Smolensk. The losses in the battle would have been no greater than the losses, up to half his total army, that Kutuzov actually sustained by pursuit over such long distances and in such atrocious weather. The death or capture of Napoleon would have been a triumph with enormous consequences. No Leipzig, no Elba, no Waterloo! A million lives saved! And Russia, instead of taking its historical place as one of several allies who brought about his downfall, would be regarded as the saviour of Europe.

Kutuzov's subordinates were meanwhile furious, and had no hesitation in expressing their impatience treacherously to St Petersburg. It says much for Kutuzov's character that he endured all this patiently. 'I can scarcely behave with common decency in his presence,' wrote Wilson. 'His feebleness outrages me to such a degree that I have declared that if he remains Commander-in-Chief, I must retire from this army.' General

Loewenstern, on Kutuzov's staff and his former admirer, was driven to exclaim retrospectively, even after victory, 'Everyone was burning with impatience to give battle. The generals and the officers protested and set fire to their tents to demonstrate that they were no longer needed; everyone awaited the signal for battle. The signal did not come. Nothing could compel Kutuzov to act. He even grew angry with those who pointed out the extent of the enemy's demoralization. . . . He kept stubbornly to his plan and advanced parallel to the enemy. He refused to take risks and preferred to expose himself to the censure of the entire army.' Bennigsen, no longer Chief-of-Staff, but still present, was even more explicit: 'Kutuzov is old, broken, sick and can barely ride. He is lazy, a womanizer and militarily ignorant. His only wish is to follow the enemy out of Russia.'

Kutuzov could not remain entirely or indefinitely deaf to this torrent of criticism, for he was in danger of losing all his authority. He agreed to slice at, more than slice off, the Napoleonic army, by cuts of a sickle more than strokes of a scythe, while he prepared, with apparent reluctance and no great sense of urgency, for its ultimate defeat at the Beresina. First he permitted a limited attack at Viasma. It was a key-point on the map because it was the junction between the routes which the two armies had hitherto been following separately. Napoleon and the Guard were the first to enter the town, on 31 October. They rested there three days, and then pressed on. But before Davout's rearguard had reached it, Miloradovich, the Russian Murat, attacked with a force of 20,000 cavalry and infantry, and cut it off from the main body by striking at the weak link between them, the civilian rabble from Moscow. The situation was saved by Eugène, next ahead, who sent back two divisions to Davout's aid. The fight continued for six hours; 4,000 French were killed or wounded, and, significantly, 3,000 taken prisoner. At the same time Ney's corps was also under attack, further west. The whole rear half of the army was in great peril, and if only Kutuzov, thirty miles further back, but within hearing of the gunfire, had possessed the will and shown the energy, the campaign might virtually have ended at Viasma. Napoleon could never have survived the loss of his three best corps.

As it was (and this was Kutuzov's extenuating motive), the

Grand Army was already fast deteriorating in strength and morale. There were three causes, which will be considered separately and can be taken to apply to the whole first part of the retreat, as far as Smolensk. These were: the mounting harassment by the Cossacks and partisans; the condition of the horses; and the physical weakening of the troops by hunger and cold.

The Cossacks became bolder as their advantage grew. The frequent forests covered their approach and withdrawal. They would burst suddenly from the trees in small groups, having watched their chance, and attack ferociously with lance and musket the straggling lines of marching men, who had no means of foreseeing their danger. Or they would wait till the enemy left the road for shelter, fuel, or food, and pounce upon them, wheeling their horses as readily through the woods as across the open plain. Their cry, 'Houra! Houra!' was heard a dozen times a day. The only means of defence was to keep the formations as tight as possible, each unit moving like a battleship firing port and starboard, fore and aft, when attacked. Or, at the halt, they would lay a powder-train to a keg of explosives, await the arrival of the Cossacks, and detonate it in their faces. When they came to a river not yet frozen firm enough to support their weight, they would hesitate on the brink before plunging in among the floes, knowing that if they did not, the Cossacks would round them up, strip them naked, and force them with prodding lances to march back as prisoners the way they had come.

From the partisans they could not expect even this small degree of mercy. Their purpose was not to take prisoners or destroy communications and supplies, as in the 1941–5 Russian war, but to kill. Kutuzov's reluctance to acknowledge their value to him or give them arms meant that they regarded themselves as free from discipline and able to commit any atrocity with impunity. Their masters, the nobility, gave them no leadership, as the Highland chieftains did in 1745. Sometimes they acted in large bands, like that, 4,000 strong, organized by Ermolay Chetvertakov, a private in a Russian regiment of dragoons, which took on an entire French battalion. More often they acted in small groups, or, sometimes, even singly, like the woman Praskovya, who defended herself with a pitchfork against six Frenchmen and killed three of them, including a colonel. Any man captured by the partisans would attempt suicide, such was the terror they inspired, and it was considered an act of mercy if a Russian officer shot him dead before the peasants could do their worst. Wilson once came upon a group of 'sixty dying, naked men whose necks were laid on a felled tree, while Russian men and women with large sticks, singing in chorus and hopping round, struck out their brains'. He saw another group of fifty buried alive, a third group burnt alive, and he considered these men fortunate to have escaped the worse tortures that awaited them. Today these atrocities have been veiled by romantic legend; at the time, the Tsar himself was moved to plead with them to modify their excesses, but his plea, coming from a place so remote from the grim reality, either was not heard or remained unheeded. There was little the French could do to stem these attacks. There were no inhabited villages which could be held to hostage, and the army was too hard pressed to send out punitive patrols.

The horses, exhausted by futile effort and constant falling, died in thousands by the road. Too weak to draw the carts with whatever reserves of food remained, they became its substitute. For hundreds of miles the army lived off horse-flesh. What fodder could be obtained was reserved for the cavalry, the gun-teams and the carriage-horses of the privileged. The rest ate pine and willow bark. It was a combination of starvation, the hardship of the march, and, soon, the ice, that destroyed them. While the ground remained soggy with rain, it required a team of six horses to drag the cannon through the mud, and more to haul them out of ditches and across ravines. Many guns were left for the Russians to tow back to Moscow as trophies; the barrels, in gleaming rows, can still be seen outside the Kremlin's arsenal. When the ground froze, it was at first of some assistance to marching men, but for the horses it was torture. Balls of impacted snow gathered in their hooves, making each step agonizing, and on the ice they found it almost impossible to remain upright. When there was a temporary thaw, and the surface water re-froze, conditions became even worse, as any motorist will testify. The Russians, from long experience, had shod their horses with winter-shoes, fitted with small iron spikes or crampons, which gave them a grip on the ice, and had exchanged wheeled vehicles for sleighs;

even the cannon were mounted on skis. In the Grand Army these precautions had been taken only by Caulaincourt for the Imperial and some of the Polish cavalry. When a band of Cossacks came upon a collapsed gun-carriage with its team dead around it, they examined first the horses' hooves, and, finding them smooth, shouted to Wilson with exhilaration that Napoleon had destroyed himself. From the loss of horses, wrote Caulaincourt, 'arose the greatest disasters of the retreat'. He may have been exaggerating. Enough horses did somehow survive in proportion to the men. Until almost the end it remained possible to mount an effective cavalry charge, and carriages more suited to Parisian boulevards crossed the Beresina.

The men suffered and died from hunger, cold and exhaustion in greater numbers than from the constant raids and the few massed attacks on their columns. They were dressed in the rags of their summer uniforms, or in motley clothes gathered from Moscow's palaces and boutiques, sometimes merchants' winter coats if they were lucky, more often absurd Tartar, Chinese, or women's furs and useless silks, their heads wrapped in multi-coloured scarves, and their feet, when boots rotted from them, in cloth and even parchment. A colonel of the artillery wrote, 'Nothing was more commonplace than to see a soldier, his face dark and repellent, wrapped in a coat of pink or blue satin, trimmed with swan or blue-fox.' The very appearance of the army, bizarre if not pathetic, lowered its pride and hope of survival.

Then came the cold. The first flurries of snow fell on 5 November. By the 7th it was falling heavily. The blizzards were so thick (like the dust after crossing the Niemen less than five months earlier) that they could not see more than fifty yards ahead or on either side. Their breath froze on their beards. The heavy weight of snow on their boots, a stone, a branch, a fallen comrade, caused constant stumbles. The snow filled and concealed cavities in the ground into which the weak would fall, some of them never to rise again. They lay there, groaning, to be covered by fresh snow in an anonymous grave, not dug decently in the earth, but built up from above as a very temporary blanket. In fine weather the glare blinded them. Only the pines stood black against the whiteness. Their lips cracked.

Their noses turned white and blue. There was no food, except dead horses, rotten vegetables – or the corpses of their friends. This is no exaggeration. Wilson saw a French soldier 'of good appearance' peeling off the charred flesh of a comrade. He asked him if this food was not loathsome to him. 'Yes,' replied the man, 'but not to save my life; only to lull the gnawing agonies.' Wilson gave him a piece of bread, and the soldier looked at him with tears of gratitude, only to fall back dead before he could eat it.

When a halt was called at nightfall, after as many as fourteen hours on the march, much of it in darkness, there was no shelter, and little rest when sentries must frequently be relieved. Their wet clothes froze on their bodies. They could seldom light a fire from frozen pine-branches, and even if they succeeded, and falling snow did not rapidly extinguish it, they knew that the flames and smell of smoke would attract the sleepless partisans. Of one company that did manage to warm themselves and roast some horse-flesh, Ségur wrote, 'In the morning they would not leave the ashes of their fires, in spite of the Russians coming up and cannon-balls already falling, saying they'd rather die than endure another day of this dreadful march.' By the time they reached Smolensk, the temperature had fallen to $-26°$ Centigrade ($-15°$ Fahrenheit). The army, which had left Maloyaroslavets 96,000 strong, arrived at Viasma with 65,000, and at Smolensk with 41,000. The road behind them had the appearance of an elongated battlefield.

The wounded suffered most. The doctors, embarrassed by their inability to give them any help, shunned them. Those who had found a place on a cart had to endure its constant jolting over rutted tracks, and their cries of anguish so exasperated the postillions that they would drive suddenly at speed to shake off their passengers to certain death under the wheels of the following cart or at the hands of partisans. Nothing illustrates more starkly the disintegration of an army's morale than indifference to its wounded. Those still sound of limb knew what their fate would be if they were wounded too, and they shirked the enemy's fire whenever they could. And nothing is more stimulating to the following enemy than to find men and baggage thrown aside to lighten the load, as if from a troika to escape the wolves. Bennigsen wrote of 'the terrible sight of stragglers at the extremities of exhaustion and starvation, ill-clad, the sick and wounded unable to walk, with death in their faces, sitting round a fire, watching the arrival of our troops without fear because they thought they couldn't suffer more than they were already suffering, gnawing the thin flesh of dead horses'. This was Wilson's recollection of the afflicting scene, day after day:

The naked masses of dead and dying men; the mangled carcasses of 10,000 horses which had in some cases been cut for food before life had ceased; the craving of famine at other points forming groups of cannibals; the air enveloped in flame and smoke; the prayers of hundreds of naked wretches flying from the peasantry, whose shouts of vengeance echoed incessantly through the woods; the wrecks of cannon, powder-waggons, all stores of every description: it formed such a scene as probably was never witnessed in the history of the world.

Napoleon preferred not to witness these horrors. He went with his Guard at the head of the column to lead them to the promised city, Smolensk, two or three days' march ahead of his rearguard. His manner was silent, grave, resigned. For most of the way he travelled in his carriage, warm in his sable cap, fur-lined greatcoat and boots. Occasionally he rode, and for short distances marched, more for the exercise than to set an example. At night his staff normally found him shelter in a building. He was reserving his energies, as any commander should, but conditions were so extreme that it is not surprising that some took this nursing of his health to be a display of indifference. Chambray wrote:

A multitude of reproaches rose against him. They blamed his ambition, which nothing could satisfy; his pride, which had made him lead them to Moscow against all the lessons of military science, and made him delay thirty-five days among its ashes. The soldiers thought only of their present misfortunes, the generals cast anxious eyes into the future.... Several cried, 'He's losing himself, and us with him!'

The private soldier, though he may be told nothing of his commander's intentions, is not slow to grasp the strategic aim, and its likely success or failure. Thiers confirms:

> He saw nothing of the retreat, and didn't want to see it, because he would have been brought face to face with the consequences of his mistakes. He preferred to deny them, and, marching two days ahead of his rearguard, not seeing their desperate state, he continued to complain of their slowness instead of going to their help.... He should have been on horseback all day supervising the passage of rivers and sustaining morale, for there was not a single death for which he was not personally responsible.

Caulaincourt was equally unforgiving:

> Never was a retreat worse planned, or carried out with less discipline.... It was to this lack of foresight that we owed a great part of our disaster. The Emperor would take no decision until the very last moment, which was invariably too late.... Constantly deluding himself with hopes of being able to call a halt and take up positions, he obstinately retained a great amount of material that ultimately caused the loss of everything.... Fortune had so often smiled on him that he could never bring himself to believe that it might prove fickle.

These judgements are harsh. As regards Napoleon's personal conduct, one could say that, having embarked upon the retreat, he was bound to lead it, not follow it. He must assure himself that Smolensk was ready to receive the army, and that the route west of it was open. Indeed there is other evidence to suggest that the men recognized this. 'They loved and clung to Napoleon as the only pilot capable of saving the ship,' wrote Tarlé, but he was speaking of the French. The Germans and the Italians are unlikely to have been so generous. Occasionally he would attempt a bitter joke. Seeing a soldier dressed in a fine fur coat, he asked him where he had stolen it. 'Sire, I bought it.' 'You mean you bought it from someone fast asleep?' The *mot* spread throughout the army, but it was taken as a licence to pillage even from comrades.

His rearguard was commanded by marshals, not colonels, men who had proved their courage, loyalty and ability in a dozen campaigns. He knew very well that his tail was under constant threat. What mattered more was the head, and, excusably, his own security. If he had remained in close touch with Ney, daily risking his life, he might marginally have encouraged the rearguard by his presence, but could have done little to improve Ney's own dispositions. Should a supreme commander always station himself at the point of crisis? Not unless the crisis is itself supreme, as it was later at the Beresina, where Napoleon was certainly not found wanting. Caulaincourt's criticism that the retreat was badly planned was justifiable. It was hardly planned at all. But that Napoleon 'would take no decision' is not. He had decided to leave Moscow. He had decided to fight Kutuzov on the Kaluga road. He had decided to break off the engagement and retreat while the weather still gave him time. His strategy might have succeeded, and nobody proposed a better one.

The army still had another hundred miles to march from Viasma to Smolensk. They managed, on average, twelve miles a day. The increasing cold was further sharpened by an evil north wind, the 'chill factor' of modern terminology, which could make two degrees of frost feel like twelve. Near Safonovo, where the road crosses a tributary of the Dnieper, there was great congestion, and the delay not only exposed them to renewed Cossack aggression, but to a mounting loss of temper as those behind reproached those in front with deliberate obstruction. The bridge was broken, the banks steep, the ice still not strong enough to bear even the weight of a man. They built another bridge; it broke; baggage was transferred to the backs of swimming horses; they drowned. At this point alone many carts were abandoned, and sixty guns.

Three items of news from the outside world reached Napoleon, all of them depressing. On 6 November he received despatches from Paris announcing the failure of the Malet conspiracy. General Claude Malet, a retired officer, had proclaimed on 23 October that Napoleon was dead and declared a provisional Republican Government. A surprising number of officers and civilian politicians believed him. Challenged by the military Governor of Paris to produce his evidence, Malet shot him dead, and placed the Minister and Prefect of Police under arrest. Loyal troops released them, seized Malet, tried and executed him. The plot was absurd and ill-planned. Malet had few fellow-conspirators, and had just escaped from a private asylum, where he had been confined after a mental breakdown. To Napoleon, however, the incident was worrying. Too many people had been prepared to believe the rumours and back this madman. 'The French are like women,' he said to Caulaincourt. 'One must not stay away from them for too long.' It was further proof to him of the danger of his isolation.

On the same day he heard of the increasing threat to his communications. Wittgenstein had succeeded in retaking Polotsk. Chichagov was approaching Minsk. If they joined forces west of Smolensk, Napoleon would face 70,000 men across his path, and about the same number in Kutuzov's army behind him. For the moment he could do little about Chichagov. The Austrians under Schwarzenberg were supposed to keep him under pressure, but they had retreated to protect Warsaw. They had done no more and no less than they had promised, to act as an auxiliary, not a main participant, and Napoleon had kept them in total ignorance of his recent misfortunes. To hold Wittgenstein, who seemed the more active and dangerous, Napoleon ordered Marshal Victor to take the offensive with his two Corps from the Vitebsk–Orsha–Smolensk region, where hitherto they had formed the army's nearest available reserve. 'The safety of the whole army depends upon you; every day's delay can mean a calamity,' wrote Berthier on the Emperor's instructions. Eugène's corps was detached from the main army to help him.

The third piece of bad news reached Napoleon on 9 November, the day he entered Smolensk. A fresh division under Barraguey d'Hilliers, marching to join the army from the south-east, had been ambushed near the city by Russian partisans, whose greatest single success this was. A complete brigade, under General Jean-Pierre Augereau, brother of the Marshal, was severely mauled, and the survivors, including their commander, surrendered. D'Hilliers had been separated from Augereau by several miles, heard the sound of firing, failed to send him help, and, when the cannonade died down, imagined that the Russians had been repulsed. But it was the silence of surrender. It was the first time that an organized body of French troops had capitulated in the course of the campaign. Augereau remained a prisoner, while d'Hilliers managed to escape with the rest of his men to Smolensk. There he encountered Napoleon, who, wild with anger, distributed what was left of his division among other formations, and sent him back to France in disgrace. He avoided the inevitable court-martial by dying two months later.

The Grand Army, whose proud name mocked their condition, slowly filtered through to Smolensk during the next two days. Having left the Niemen half a million strong, and Moscow with 100,000, it was now reduced to 41,000. For weeks they had looked forward to rest, shelter and abundant supplies in the city. In all three they were disappointed.

CHAPTER SEVEN

THE DNIEPER AND THE BERESINA

Napoleon and his Guard were the first to reach Smolensk again. He remained there four days, 9–12 November, and the last of the rearguard did not struggle in until the day he left.

The strategic pattern was tightening as the outer Russian armies came to play an important role in the centre (see maps on pages xii and 136). In the very far north Macdonald had abandoned the siege of Riga, sent back the siege-train to Danzig, and, having no orders from Napoleon to do anything else, vaguely, ineffectually and unhappily occupied a vast stretch of frozen country between the Dvina and the Niemen, and played virtually no further part in the campaign except to leave it in an ignominious manner at the end. Wittgenstein, ignoring him, moved south to capture Vitebsk on 7 November, and then was temporarily blocked by Oudinot and Victor in the gap between the Dvina and the Dnieper. The Russian central army, directly under Kutuzov, was moving through Elnia in a wide southern sweep round Smolensk to cut the Smolensk–Orsha road at Krasnoe. On 16 November Chichagov captured Minsk with its huge quantity of stores, and was advancing on Borisov, the essential bridgehead on the Beresina. Schwarzenberg, far to the south-west round Brest-Litovsk, had, like Macdonald, no further effective contribution to make. So Napoleon was faced at Smolensk with the probability that his single route to safety would be barred, perhaps at the Dnieper crossing at Orsha, or seventy miles further west on the Beresina, by three converging Russian armies, and, if he was to escape the trap, he must hurry.

He should, of course, have left Smolensk almost as soon as he entered it. But this was not possible, because he had promised his men at least a temporary haven where they could rest and eat, and he must wait until the rearguard had caught up. 'Rest' was a euphemism. The city was in ruins from the earlier battle, and although the Dnieper bridge had been rebuilt and some of the sturdier buildings shored up, it was still a place that stank of death, and the troops camped mostly under canvas amid the rubble. 'Eat' was a travesty of what had been promised. The city had been quite well stocked since its capture in August. Supplies had steadily moved to it from Germany and Poland, including cattle on the hoof, and wines and delicacies from France. Some stores had been forwarded to Moscow, but much was consumed by the troops who brought them, much more taken away by Victor's and Oudinot's corps when they were ordered north. The rest was gobbled up within three days by the first arrivals from the east, Napoleon's Guard. There was no proper system of distribution. First come, served themselves. In vain the quartermasters appealed for rationing, for requisitions signed by an officer, for authorized sergeants to draw the entitlement for their battalions. But paper-work of this kind was intolerable to starving and exhausted men. They broke into the warehouses. They ate their fill before distributing to their comrades what remained. They gave no thought to the thousands who had yet to reach the city. It was a situation familiar in all wars, that front-line troops despise administrative troops for their security and comfort, and, when suddenly brought face to face with them in a crisis, treat their orders with contumely, and have the strength and psychological advantage to ignore them.

Napoleon, realizing the uselessness of protest and wishing to nurse his Guards, turned on the Governor of Smolensk, General Charpentier, with bitter reproaches that the city was not better supplied. The Governor had many reasonable excuses. He was not responsible for despatching stores, only for receiving and distributing them. He had not been told of the Grand Army's state of debilitation, and had heard of its approach only a day or two before. He had prepared Smolensk as a base, not as a place of refuge for the entire army. He had not been forewarned that stragglers, and then Victor, would remove half his cherished

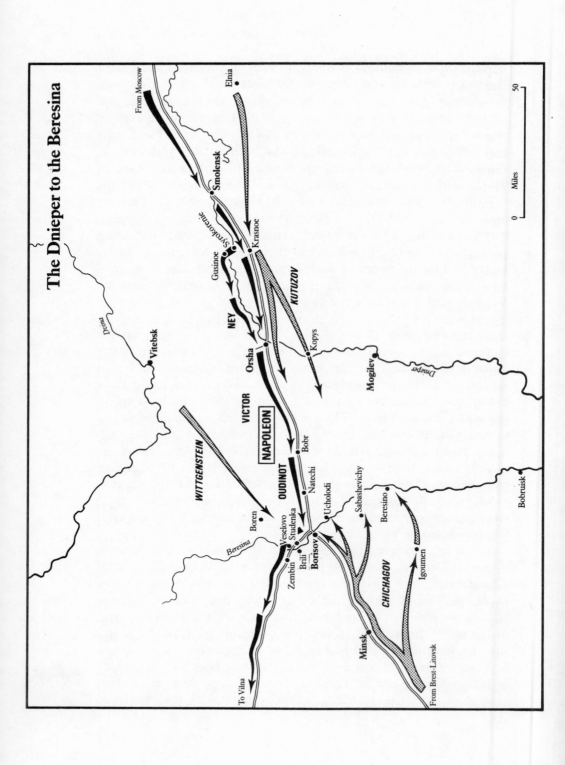

The Dnieper to the Beresina

From Moscow

Elnia

Smolensk

Syrokorenie

Gusinoe

Krasnoe

NEY

KUTUZOV

Kopys

Orsha

Vitebsk

Dvina

Mogilev

Dnieper

VICTOR

WITTGENSTEIN

NAPOLEON

Bobr

OUDINOT

Natechi

Ucholodi

Boren

Sabashevichy

Beresino

Bobruisk

Veselovo

Studenka

Beresina

Zembin

Briii

Borisov

CHICHAGOV

Igoumen

To Vilna

Minsk

From Brest-Litovsk

0   Miles   50

supplies. Then came the undisciplined Guards, the envied of
the army because they were considered its élite and had not
fought a single battle, and they were allowed to take first pick
of the stores. It was inhuman. The gates were closed against
the others, who had borne the brunt of the campaign and protected the advance guard. Now they broke in, ransacked the
town, got drunk on brandy, and many of them found a hap-
pier death inebriated than sober in Cossack hands. 'Thus',
commented Ségur, 'do great expeditions collapse under their own
weight.'

The Emperor, having stifled his anger, behaved as if there was
no crisis. He lodged in an intact building in the Place Neuve,
and rode out every day to inspect the city and its defences, as if
he expected to remain there. His impassivity was simulated, but
it impressed the men. He ignored the markets set up in the
squares to sell to the inhabitants, and to officers who felt no
shame, the booty of Moscow. Then he decided to leave.

The Guard was to form the spear-head, the remainder of the
army to follow when they had destroyed the city walls. Ney was
to command the rearguard. The Grand Army now numbered
about 40,000. The artillery had already lost 350 guns, and
the cavalry was down to 3,000. With the detachment of Victor's corps and the destruction of d'Hilliers' division, no reinforcements reached them in Smolensk, apart from a few
hundred recruits who arrived, exhausted, after marching from
France.

Napoleon led the army westwards towards Orsha, on the same
road he had marched so effortlessly on the way to Moscow. Now
it was winter. Gentle slopes which had then seemed insignificant
now presented major obstacles. They were slippery sheets of ice,
even more dangerous on the descent than on the ascent. The
road was so polished by those in front that those behind 'slid on
their posteriors' (Caulaincourt), including Napoleon himself,
supported by his retainers. The staff-officers were obliged to
dismount and lead their horses by the bridle. On the first day
the Guard took twenty-two hours to cover fifteen miles. Many
carriages and carts were destroyed to spare the horses. The
officers ceased trying to impose order, knowing that disorder
would immediately be resumed, and the distinction between

ranks was slowly eroded. A grimly humorous example is quoted by Major von Lossberg. A private soldier thought his officer dead, and began to strip him of his warmer clothes. The officer, barely audible, whispered, '*Camarade, je ne suis pas encore mort.*' The soldier stood aside: '*Eh bien, mon officier, j'attendrai encore quelques moments.*'

The days were short, light by 8 am, dark by 4. When they reached their bivouacs, the men were often lost, crying out the names and numbers of their regiments. Many fell asleep after fruitless search, and woke to find the army gone and themselves at the mercy of the Cossacks who were always on their flanks. The cold killed many of them overnight. Baron Larrey, chief surgeon to the army, noticed that the bald died first. If they managed to light a fire, so many crowded round it that front seats were sold for high prices, and if they went too close to it, and then returned to the cold, their noses and fingers turned gangrenous. Many who swallowed snow to quench their thirst perished when it reached their intestines. Wine and coffee were the best sedatives, but rarely obtained. As they could seldom halt to kill and quarter the horses for food, they cut steaks from their haunches as they slithered along, and the horses gave no sign of pain, being numbed by cold. The wounds congealed instantly in 16 degrees of frost, but later they formed pus, and the horses died.

One personal experience of this terrible march (but not the most terrible, because worse was to follow) was recorded by the actress, Louise Fusil. She still had her coach, but found herself among the stragglers, men who had lost their regiments or deserted them, and had thrown away their weapons, stealing, shirking, in order to survive. She and her escort came to a ravine which was made impassable by its icy steepness and Cossack fire from the far bank. They left the coach, mounted horses, and rode belly-deep in snow across the fields. It was midnight on 14 November. They halted, not knowing where they were. The officers with her said gaily that they were bound to be captured next day. They could not light a fire for fear of attracting Cossacks. 'I then experienced a moment of discouragement,' wrote Louise retrospectively, with proud understatement. At 4 am they continued west, guided by the sound of cannon-fire. They regained the road. Her coach, to her astonishment, caught up with her. Wounded men begged a lift. It was refused. At dawn the coachman said that the horses were too exhausted to go any further. She continued on foot, seeking Napoleon's headquarters, entered Krasnoe, found it on fire. She resigned herself to die. She felt the cold stifling her, but remembered that someone had told her that it was an easy death. She lost consciousness. A soldier found her in the snow, carried her to a peasant's hut and wrapped her in furs. An officer brought her a mug of coffee, and told her to keep it 'as an historic souvenir for your family', but added under his breath, 'if you ever see them again'. The officer was Dr Desgenettes, the famous Inspector General of the Medical Services, and the coffee was brewed by Marshal Lefebvre, commander of the infantry of the Old Guard. She was indeed fortunate in her rescuers. She recovered sufficiently to continue in her coach towards the Beresina.

Krasnoe was the site of a running battle which lasted for four days against different Corps of the army. One must imagine it as a train of self-propelled coaches unattached to the engine. The engine was Napoleon, in front with the Guard. Behind came Eugène's corps, returned from his foray north to aid Victor; then Davout's; finally Ney's, the rearguard, which was still in Smolensk. The whole line extended forty miles. First, a force of 20,000 under Miloradovich cut the road between Napoleon and Eugène, six miles east of Krasnoe. Heavily outnumbered, Eugène fought back, and Napoleon sent two regiments of the Young Guard to help him. The Russians unaccountably broke off the action. 'Being so unused to victory,' wrote Ségur in an untypically Tacitean phrase, 'they knew not how to make use of it.' During the night Eugène led his corps through the moonlit snowfields north of the road. Once they were challenged, but a Russian-speaking Pole replied that they were a Russian corps 'on a secret mission', and the whole body passed through safely to Krasnoe. They were obliged to leave behind them a great quantity of stores, including the huge cross of Ivan's tower in Moscow which Napoleon had intended to erect over the Invalides, brought so far (with what muttered curses one can imagine) and now abandoned, and Davout's carriage, with his maps of India and his Marshal's baton, and military chests containing gold and silver ingots and over £200,000 in coin. All this, amid dreadful scenes of carnage, was witnessed by Sir Robert Wilson next day.

Davout and Ney were still east of the Russian road-block. The enemy pressed so close to Krasnoe that the French could see into their camps, and contemptuously observed their evening rituals. The relics of the Moscow saints were brought out for the adoration of the soldiers. 'The priests fanaticized these recruits by exhortations which seemed ridiculous and barbaric to our civilized people' (Ségur). But however ridiculous, Napoleon could not ignore the danger that these men posed to the rear half of the army. For the first time in the campaign he ordered the Old Guard into action. On 17 November, 16,000 strong, under General Roguet and with Napoleon himself in close attendance ('I've played the role of Emperor too long; now it's time to be a General again'), they returned east and south from Krasnoe, and the opposition melted away. Colonel Davidov's description is famous, and cautions us against assuming that the Guard's morale and discipline had disintegrated:

The Old Guard approached with Napoleon himself among them. We jumped on our horses and again appeared on the highway.... The enemy, noticing our noisy crew, cocked their guns and went on proudly marching without accelerating their step. No matter how hard we tried to detach at least one private from these closed columns, they remained unharmed, as though made of granite, disdaining all our efforts. I shall never forget the easy gait and the impressive bearing of these warriors, inured to all manner of deaths. In their tall bearskin caps, blue uniforms with white straps and red plumes and epaulettes, they looked like poppies amid the snowy fields. Having only Cossacks at our disposal, we buzzed round the passing enemy columns, capturing waggons and guns that lagged behind, sometimes breaking up a scattered or extended platoon, but the columns themselves remained unscathed. Colonels, officers, sergeants, many privates rushed at the enemy, but all in vain. The columns moved on, one after another, driving us off with shots from their rifles and jeering at our futile attempts to raid them.... Napoleon and the

Guard passed through our Cossacks like a hundred-gun warship through fishing-boats.

The road remained open for Davout, but not for Ney.

It was on this very day that Ney marched out of Smolensk. He had not been left undisturbed to carry out the demolitions which Napoleon had ordered. The St Petersburg suburb north of the Dnieper had been under repeated attack by Cossacks. Fezensac, who was in command there, attempted to withdraw his men over the bridge, but, finding the approaches too congested, led them back to face their pursuers, and drove them through the snow-covered ruins with the bayonet, watched and applauded by Ney from the battlements on the south bank. Segur quotes this incident as an example of how spiritual qualities triumph over physical distress. When a man's instinct is to fly, he is rallied by the very mention of his honour. 'Why? What is the glory to a rifleman who dies without witnesses, is not commended or mourned except by his platoon? But the same emotions which are excited in a general by his army are excited in a private by his section.'

A gap of twenty miles had now opened between Ney and Davout. There had been some misunderstanding of orders, some failure of communication between them, with the result that Davout left Smolensk a day too early, or Ney a day too late, and the Russian road-block which the Old Guard had swept aside was now even more firmly fixed across his path. Ney does not seem to have considered the alternative of marching along the north bank of the Dnieper to avoid it, possibly because the tracks were too bad or he did not know that the gap between him and Davout was so wide and filled by the enemy. He left Smolensk on 17 November on the Krasnoe road with 6,000 men in organized units and many thousands of stragglers, but could not take with him the sick and wounded, of whom some 5,000 were left in the city, 'like outworn tools', says Chambray. He reached the Krasnoe battlefield at 3 pm on the 18th and found it occupied by Miloradovich. This time Napoleon could send no help. It had become too urgent to press on to the Beresina, and on the day of Ney's great crisis, the Emperor was already at Orsha. He assumed that the Marshal, the hero of the campaign, must be accounted lost. 'He will attempt the impossible, and lose his life in some desperate attack. I'd give 330 million in gold to save him.' It was said that he would return through Kiev rather than surrender. The actual event was even more remarkable. Ney's achievement was the most astonishing of the campaign.

His advance guard met the Russian batteries head-on. Three enemy Corps closed behind him and on each side. Miloradovich sent an officer under a flag of truce to invite his surrender, telling him that Napoleon had deserted him, and that he would not make such a proposal to so famous a marshal if his desperate situation were not obvious to both of them. Ney replied, 'A marshal does not surrender.' At that moment some shots rang out and a few Frenchmen fell. Protesting that this was a breach of the truce, Ney held the Russian officer prisoner, not wishing him to return to Miloradovich with details of the corps' pitiful condition. Miloradovich had not been exaggerating. Kutuzov had concentrated almost his entire army at this point, some 80,000 men, and his guns dominated the road. Ney first attempted to break through with 3,000. They pierced the first Russian line, and were advancing on the second when a hail of rifle and artillery fire halted them. They retired to a ravine, and re-formed, astonished that Kutuzov did not come down from the hills to attack them directly. Kutuzov's caution was deliberate: he believed that he could force Ney's surrender by gun-fire alone.

At 4 pm it grew dark. Ney momentarily considered a retreat to Smolensk, if that were possible, but changed his mind because there was no security there and the psychological effect on his men would have been disastrous. He now determined to find a way across the Dnieper and reach Orsha along its north bank. Lighting camp-fires to conceal his move, he set off into the unknown. He had only one map, on too small a scale to guide him cross-country, but he found a stream flowing north, and led his men along a track parallel to it. They came across a peasant, who told them that the river was three miles ahead, but there was no ford there and the water would be unfrozen: there had been a slight thaw. The man led them to the river bank at the village of Syrokorenie. It was true that the Dnieper was not frozen bank to bank, but by great good fortune the drift-ice had jammed at a bend in the river, and it was just possible, by leaping from floe to floe, to cross it. An officer tested it, reached the far bank with difficulty, and signalled the others on. The crossing began at midnight. Under the first troops the ice began to sway, and there was a constant sound of grinding and cracking. They widened their distances apart, and about 2,000 men managed to cross, and a few horses by swimming. The six remaining cannon and all the vehicles were abandoned, together with some 3,000 other troops and 4,000 stragglers, including women and children, and the non-walking wounded.

It was still forty-five miles to Orsha. They followed the river bank to a village called Gusinoe, where to their delight they found some food, and a hundred Cossacks asleep, whom they took prisoner with their horses. Pressing onwards in the dawn they came under observation, but not at first under attack, by a much larger body of Cossacks. Ney led his men from wood to wood, keeping as close as possible to the river, and they marched all that day and all the next night. The Cossacks now became more aggressive, under the direct command of Platov, and they had cannon with them which raked the French column, now reduced by casualties and the exhaustion of the march to 1,500 men. Some of them cried in despair that they must surrender. Ney replied by pointing in one direction to France, in the other to captivity. They crossed ravines and minor tributaries waist-deep in half-frozen water, using the main river to maintain direction. At another village they rested for a few hours, were soon discovered there by the Cossacks, and, forming squares, held off the attacks till nightfall. At 9 pm Ney resumed the march, and felt that he was now close enough to Orsha to risk sending ahead a handful of his remaining horsemen to summon help, not knowing whether Orsha was still in friendly hands. It was. Three miles from the town they were challenged, in French. Eugène himself was there. He had received Ney's message. They fell into each other's arms, and entered Orsha together at 5 am on 21 November, with the 800 men who survived from the 6,000 who had fought at Krasnoe.

When Napoleon, twelve miles west of Orsha, heard the news, he could hardly contain himself for joy. He dubbed Ney 'the bravest of the brave', a title which still hangs round his name like a medal. It was his personal survival that counted, the example of fortitude that he had set to the whole army. In the euphoria of the moment, it was overlooked that his corps had virtually ceased to exist. All that Ney wished for was to find Davout, and load him with imprecations for abandoning him.

News of the Grand Army's fate was beginning to trickle through to the outside world. When Paris heard that they had left Moscow, there was no great alarm, because they trusted Napoleon's genius and imagined a great manoeuvre which would bring him out of Russia with honour. Privately Napoleon told his ministers the grim truth. On 18 November he wrote to Maret, his Minister of Foreign Affairs, who was in Vilna:

> Our position has grown worse. Almost all our horses – 30,000 of them – have perished as a result of the cold, 16 degrees of frost. We have had to burn more than 300 guns and a huge number of ammunition waggons. The cold weather has greatly increased the number of stragglers. The Cossacks have taken advantage of our complete lack of cavalry, and almost complete lack of artillery, to harass us and cut our communications, so that I am anxious about Marshal Ney, who stayed behind with 3,000 [sic] men to blow up Smolensk. Otherwise, given a few days' rest, some good food, and, above all, some horses and a supply of artillery, we shall still make good. The enemy have one thing we lack – they are accustomed to moving on ice, and this gives them an immense advantage over us. A gun or an ammunition waggon that we cannot drag out of an insignificant ravine without losing 12 or 15 horses, and 12 to 15 hours, they can haul up by using sledges and other apparatus made for the purpose, as rapidly as if there was no ice at all.

On 23 November he called Caulaincourt for another of their intimate talks. Two days earlier he had received the news that Minsk had fallen to Chichagov. It was hardly the fault of Bronikovsky, whose division held it: he had only 4,000 men against 30,000. But it was a terrible loss, because Minsk contained enough stores to feed the entire army throughout the winter; but more important, because it put a Russian army directly across his path. He seemed to Caulaincourt, for the first time, severely shaken. 'This is beginning to be very serious,' he said. He asked whether the lakes and rivers would be frozen hard enough to support artillery. Caulaincourt doubted it. If they could cross the Beresina, Napoleon went on, they would be safe enough, because between the Vistula and the Niemen he could count on 30,000 fresh troops in the fortresses, excluding the Austrians, and with them he might hold the Beresina as a winter line. 'If not, we shall try what our pistols can do.' He gave orders that all unnecessary equipment should be burnt, including the bridging-train, as he expected to seize and hold the vital bridge at Borisov. Then he dozed off. Daru and Duroc remained behind to talk. Napoleon woke up and asked what they were saying. 'We were wishing that we had a balloon.' 'What for?' 'To carry off Your Majesty.' It was more than a joke, because the Emperor had been saying to Caulaincourt that he must return to Paris, and Caulaincourt was to go with him.

It was not until the next day that he heard that Chichagov had captured the Borisov bridge on 21 November. He had force-marched his army in three columns from Minsk, the southern one via Igoumen to Beresino, the central corps on Ucholodi and Sabashevichy higher up the Beresina, and the third on Borisov itself, which he captured from Bronikovsky after a day-long battle. The majority of the Polish and Württemberg troops escaped across the river, but the town, which lay on the east bank, fell too, and Chichagov was able to push patrols along the main road towards Natechi, where he was stopped by Oudinot. It was the same audacious manoeuvre as the 18th Panzer Division achieved on 2 July 1941, when they streaked from Minsk to Borisov, hurled aside the Russian defenders, and captured the bridge intact. The difference was that Oudinot immediately counter-attacked. He managed to recapture the town, and take 800 prisoners, six cannon and much baggage, but as he advanced to the bridge, which was an exceptionally long wooden structure, the Russians set fire to it in three places, and retired to hold the bluffs that overlooked it from the western side of the river. It was impossible to repair it under intense gunfire.

The army was slowly moving up from Orsha towards Bobr. Conditions were a little better. The thaw which had nearly trapped Ney on the Dnieper was at first a relief after the intense cold, because the men could sleep a little. They were re-entering country which was not historically Russian, and the population, if not friendly, at least did not burn their villages and their stores, or murder the exhausted troops. At Orsha they had even found enough food in the warehouses to feed 40,000 men for two days. The improvement, however, was marginal and temporary. Marching through mud was more tiring than on impacted snow. A Prussian officer, Count Johann von Borcke, wrote of this stage of the march: 'Gloomy, silent, and with downcast gaze, this rabble of dying men walked from Orsha to the Beresina like a funeral procession.... We had sunk to the level of animals.' When Victor first saw the army, on returning to the main road with his corps, he was appalled by their spectral appearance, 'without shame, without arms, bearded, units mixed up, eyes on ground, silent, like a gang of prisoners'. He was most deeply shocked by the sight of colonels and even generals thinking only of themselves, with no troops under their command, marching mingled with the common soldiers, who paid no attention to them. Napoleon ordered all stragglers to return to their units, threatening officers who disobeyed with demotion, and soldiers with death, but this had little effect, when death was the one thing that many of them craved. They heard of the loss of Vitebsk, Minsk and now Borisov, with an instinctive understanding of what it meant. The name of the Beresina, which had seemed so insignificant a stream on their advance to Moscow, was now on all their lips.

Napoleon turned over in his mind and in conversation the various alternatives open to him. He could make a do-or-die attempt to recapture and re-build the Borisov bridge. He could force a crossing downstream, at Beresino, for instance, and retake Minsk. He could strike north-west from the main road to find a rumoured ford near Veselovo, or bypass the river entirely by ascending above its head-waters, as he had done in July, and make for Vilna. For a time he favoured the first (Minsk) plan, but abandoned it because the river widened as it flowed south, and Chichagov was already in position to stop him. The northern plan was tempting: Napoleon brightened when he conceived the fantasy of trapping Wittgenstein and leading his army captive back to Paris. He called it 'a lovely manoeuvre'. But this plan was also discarded because it would be too long a march on wretched roads, and Wittgenstein might easily enter Vilna before him. It seemed that the direct approach through Borisov gave him the best chance of escaping the trap, but it would mean a very costly battle. His assets were three: that in Victor's and Oudinot's corps he had two strong formations (in all about 20,000 men) which were relatively fresh, as neither had made the march to Moscow and back. Secondly, that Kutuzov's lethargy and lack of unifying control made it unlikely that the Grand Army would be pressed very hard from behind, or that the three Russian armies would operate together well enough to close every exit. The third advantage was Napoleon's reputation. Twice already, at Viasma and Krasnoe, the enemy had failed to use their superior strength, and it can only have been due to the fear that he still inspired, that genius, as Wellington had said, which made his presence on a battlefield worth 40,000 men.

Then, late on 24 November, he received news which gave him renewed hope. A French officer, Brigadier-General Corbineau, in command of a regiment of cavalry which was coming south by a roundabout route from Polotsk, reached Borisov and found it in enemy hands. He turned back up the river through the forests, and saw a mounted Lithuanian peasant fording the river opposite a village called Studenka, seven miles north of Borisov. The man was seized, and showed them that the water was only three feet deep, except in the middle, for a distance of about twelve feet, where horses had to swim. It was the same ford which Charles XII had found in 1708. Corbineau rode into the water with his 600 men, and although the current was strong and there was much floating ice, all but twenty crossed safely. On the far side he turned south and joined Oudinot, to whom he told his story, and Oudinot immediately told Napoleon, who sent for him at Bobr.

He questioned him closely about his discovery. Corbineau estimated that the river was about 100 yards wide at that point, and although cavalry could pass with difficulty, as he himself had done, infantry would be swept away when they reached the central channel and drown in the ice-cold water. The river was deepening, and the current increasing, every hour with melting snow. It could not, at this time of year, be reckoned a ford at all. It must be bridged. There was the further difficulty that there were marshes on each side, passable on foot in frosty weather, but, if the present thaw continued, risky for infantry and impossible for wheeled vehicles. At the moment the ground was stiff but not frozen. It could harden further, or soften. On the west bank there was no proper road until Zembin, only a causeway with many trestled bridges, which could easily be destroyed ahead of them, and there was no other way across the marsh unless it froze solid. Paradoxically, it was the thaw, not the cold, that nearly ended Napoleon's career on the Beresina. In late November the river and its marshes were normally frozen hard, and he could have crossed almost anywhere.

Corbineau's report was sufficiently optimistic for Napoleon to order Oudinot to occupy Studenka immediately with an infantry regiment and Corbineau's cavalry, and his chief engineer, General Eblé, to hurry there next morning, the 25th. The plan had the advantage that the west bank was not held by Chichagov in strength, but was watched by a light Cossack patrol at Brili. Wittgenstein was still thirty miles to the north-east, and Kutuzov even further off, at Kopys on the Dnieper, three days' march behind. The Grand Army could slip between them and make for Vilna. It was of the greatest importance that Chichagov should continue to believe that Napoleon intended to attempt a crossing between Borisov and Beresino, and to lure his Cossacks away from the Studenka bridge site. Deceptively ostentatious preparations were made at Ucholodi, Sabashevichy and Borisov itself. Trees were noisily felled, sawn and hammered at each place to simulate bridge-building, and several hundred stragglers, who at last found a new role, acted as decoy troops for the benefit of Chichagov's spies. Victor would hold off Wittgenstein, and Davout would watch Kutuzov. Napoleon himself now had about 40,000 effective troops, and the same number of unarmed stragglers. It seemed unlikely that many of the latter could be saved. The fighting men must be given priority. He marched west from Bobr towards Borisov to maintain for as long as possible the fiction that he was about to force a passage there or further south, and then overnight, 25/26 November, switched north to Studenka.

His deception plan worked well. Chichagov, on the instructions of Kutuzov, who had little idea what was happening but was convinced that Napoleon wanted to recapture Minsk, spread his army widely below Borisov to guard every possible river-crossing, but kept his main force at Borisov itself, from where he could deploy rapidly right or left. During the critical days 24 and 25 November, the only move he made was in the wrong direction, to strengthen his position at Sabashevichy, drawing more troops from Borisov.

He greatly overestimated Napoleon's strength, believing that with Victor's and Oudinot's corps he now had 100,000 men under command, the same number with which he had left Moscow, not realizing that half the men were unarmed and disorganized, for he had not seen with his own eyes the evidence of their shattered condition which they left behind them on each mile of road. Consequently, he thought himself vastly outnumbered, and his army spread much too thin. Bennigsen, in his memoirs, asserts that this was indeed true, and that if Napoleon had taken the Minsk route he would have had little trouble in breaking through. Chichagov was blamed undeservedly for Napoleon's escape. He was the only one of the three Russian army-commanders to be in position in accordance with the master strategy. He was given an impossible task – to cover the whole river-line with an inferior force.

Meanwhile, his small Cossack detachment at Brili did their duty by reporting unusual French activity at Studenka, but their warning came too late. Little can they have realized that the issue of the whole campaign depended upon the sharpness of their eyes and the speed of their couriers.

Napoleon's chief engineer, General Eblé, to whom is due more than any other man, even Napoleon, the credit for the miracle of the Beresina, arrived at Studenka on the morning of 25 November. All the pontoon bridges had been destroyed by the Emperor's order at Orsha, and Eblé had to manufacture two bridges out of what timbers he could tear from the houses at Studenka and Veselovo. There was no time to fell trees and shape them. Fortunately he had had the good sense to exempt from the Emperor's destruction order several forges, chests of tools, and cart-loads of scrap-iron from wheels of abandoned gun-carriages, with which he managed to make crampons to hold the timbers together. His sappers set to work immediately. There were to be two bridges, each 300 feet long, one of lighter construction for the infantry, on which they began first, and the second for cavalry, artillery and vehicles, 200 yards downstream. Both were trestle bridges, their supports resting in the muddy bed of the river, and both were surfaced by rough planking and fascines. On the stronger bridge, moss and straw were laid to give the horses purchase and to minimize the vibration of the waggons passing over them.

The trestles, twenty-three for each bridge, were made during the night under cover of the river bank to deaden the sound of hammering from any Russian patrols that might be opposite. At dawn on 26 November they were carried to the waterside, and rammed in at increasing depths by men working waist-deep at first, then up to their necks, for hours on end. The deep central channel was bridged by the engineers working from rafts. In the minds of all who witnessed the operation remained the amazing gallantry of the 400 men who executed it, and Eblé's personal encouragement of them. He told them, which was indeed the truth, that the fate of the Grand Army depended upon them. Few of them survived. They either died of frost-bite where they stood among the ice-floes, were swept downstream, or were killed when the vehicle bridge broke and they re-entered the river to repair it under heavy fire.

By 1 pm on 26 November, the first, infantry, bridge was ready, and the vehicle bridge by 4 that afternoon. A few men had crossed the river before this to protect the sappers from any enemy who might be lurking on the far bank. The first was Oudinot's aide-de-camp, Jacquinot, who swam the river on horseback, found a few Cossacks, took one of them prisoner, and returned with him, riding pillion, across the stream. The man said that Chichagov had moved south of Borisov, leaving at Brili only a light patrol. Napoleon exclaimed with delight that he had duped the Admiral (which was Chichagov's official rank). What seems inexplicable is that the visible massing of the French troops at Studenka, and the construction of the bridges, had not been reported to him sooner.

The next to cross the river was a troop of Polish Lancers, and 400 infantry on two rafts, which made twenty trips. Then Oudinot led his corps across on the completed infantry bridge and formed a protective screen on the opposite bank. They found the Cossacks thinly spread, with a couple of guns, and brushed them aside without difficulty. All that afternoon (26 November) the infantry divisions passed across as fast as they reached Studenka, and then the long convoy of vehicles and guns joined them as soon as the heavy bridge was ready. By the evening, Davout's and Eugène's corps were safely across. They all congratulated themselves on their good fortune. The first setback came with the buckling of the heavy bridge, which caused an interruption of several hours before it could be repaired. At 2 am next morning it again collapsed, and the sappers returned to the water for four more hours. As the pressure of arriving troops, stragglers and civilians mounted at the bridgehead, and the delays grew longer, there were inevitable conflicts for priority. Formations, units and individuals insisted that the fate of the army depended upon their survival, and if this was scarcely credible, they pushed themselves forward with the energy of despair.

Two examples will stand for many such incidents. Louise Fusil, now installed in the carriage of Marshal Lefebvre, used her protector's authority to force her way to the front. At the approach to the vehicle bridge she saw Napoleon, 'looking as calm as at a review at the Tuileries'. He said to her, 'Go on, go on. Don't be frightened. There is no need to fear.' She also saw Murat, who saluted her ('He was a flirt, and liked women to notice him'). The horses had to be led. The bridge was so fragile that it trembled under the carriage-wheels. But she crossed the river safely, and eventually arrived back in Paris to spend the rest of her life lecturing increasingly indifferent audiences on how she crossed the Beresina.

The other example, recorded by Fezensac, was less aristocratic. A woman canteen-keeper, who had borne a child in Prussia before the campaign, followed the 33rd Regiment all the way to Moscow with her infant daughter. They survived the retreat miraculously. The mother fed the girl with horses' blood, and wrapped her in Moscow furs. Twice she lost her, then found her again, once in a field, then in a burnt cottage. The mother crossed the Beresina on a horse, with water up to her neck, holding the bridle in one hand, and in the other the child above her head. They both survived the remainder of the march. The girl did not even catch cold.

This anguished passage was not to last for long unopposed. On 28 November both bridgeheads came under strong Russian attack. Wittgenstein on the east bank, and Chichagov on the west, realized that they must move quickly to prevent Napoleon's escape. Wittgenstein in his advance south had not been informed of what was happening at Studenka, and bypassed it by an easier route to make direct for Borisov. Nearing the town, he encountered a division under the command of General Partouneaux, which had been left there as rearguard, and was now attempting to make its way north to Studenka. His small force was no match for Wittgenstein's 20,000 and a section of Chichagov's army coming up behind him. Caught between them in snow-filled forests, he refused to surrender, but next morning, the 28th, he acknowledged that his situation was desperate. He capitulated with the 500 men under his immediate command, and his two other brigades, hearing the news, surrendered too, a total of 4,000 men. Only one of his battalions succeeded in reaching Studenka. It was a greater humiliation than d'Hilliers', the only division throughout the campaign to surrender *en masse*. Napoleon, thinking of Ney in a similar situation, never forgave him. Partouneaux survived his imprisonment, returned to France to enjoy a long political and military career, and died of apoplexy in 1835.

More serious was Chichagov's long-delayed attack towards the western bridgehead, and Wittgenstein's on the eastern. The Grand Army was taking three days to cross the Beresina. By this time it was split between the two banks, Napoleon with the Guard, who had crossed at midday on the 27th, with Ney's and Davout's corps on the home-side, Victor's on the other. Napoleon was urged by Ney to burn the bridges, but he refused to isolate Victor. He insisted that both banks be held until all the organized formations were over. During 28 November there was a fierce battle on both banks to hold them. On the west, Oudinot and Davout beat back the Russians by infantry and cavalry charges, when Oudinot was badly wounded. On the east bank,

Victor, now encircled in a tight perimeter, managed, just, to hold his position, and cross the river with his corps during the night, cutting his way through the refugees with swords. At 10 in the morning of the 29th, Eblé set fire to both bridges. The fires ran quickly from end to end, while some were still trying to cross. A cry of despair rose from those stranded on the far bank.

The tragedy was that the vast, second, army of stragglers and civilians (call them collectively non-combatants) were abandoned, in all some 30,000. They had not taken advantage of their chances. During the two nights, 27/28 and 28/29 November, many of them could have crossed the bridges, but they refused to leave their camp-fires. In daylight, pounded by Russian artillery, which was now on the banks above them, they clustered so thickly on the bridge approaches, *ripae ulterioris amore*, that few could squeeze through, and priority was given to the troops. Ségur describes the scene:

They ran in every direction. They accumulated on the bank. In a second one saw a huge mass, men, horses, carts, laying siege to the narrow entrances to the bridges. Those in front, pushed by those behind, pushed back by the guards and the sappers, or stopped by the river, thrown down, or trampled on, or hurled into the freezing river. From this huge and terrible throng rose a ghastly cry, now a low humming, now a great shout, mingled with moans and terrible curses.... Some cut a way for their waggons with sabres. Others collapse, weep, despair. Some, shoved away from the bridges, try to climb its sides, but most are pushed into the river. Women with children in their arms among the floes hold up their little ones while they drown. Then the artillery bridge collapses. Those on it try to retreat; those behind don't know of the collapse, and pushed forward, shoving those in front into the gap and falling into it themselves. They then swarm to the other bridge. They think themselves safe on setting foot on the bridge, but a fallen horse, a plank missing, breaks the flow. On the far side the marsh, the barrier, prevents free passage. On the bridge itself, fighting for a foothold, many are forced into the river, for there were no guard-rails on the bridge.

They refused to acknowledge that one bridge was reserved for pedestrians, the other for vehicles, and they assaulted both. When told that the lighter bridge would not bear the weight of vehicles, they paid no attention. Prevented by bayonets from advancing, some flung themselves into the river and tried to swim across. Few succeeded. Some clung to ice-floes, but they were carried downstream to drown. When the bridges were set on fire, some tried to dash through the flames. The army witnessed all this with horror from the far bank. Then the Cossacks descended among them, and killed even the women and children.

It is uncertain how many crossed the Beresina. Perhaps 30,000. But Napoleon lost 25,000 in battle casualties, and as many more among non-combatants. He had about 20,000 men left, organized effectively to fight again. They gained the Zembin causeway, unaccountably left intact by Chichagov, and made as much speed as they could towards Vilna.

How had Napoleon escaped? He had had two strokes of good fortune. A sudden frost had succeeded the thaw at a critical moment, freezing the marshes on the left bank of the Beresina firmly enough for men and vehicles to approach the bridges, and on the far side to reach the Zembin causeway. His second blessing was the incompetence of his opponents. The Russian plan had been a fine strategic conception. Had it been better executed, the French would have been destroyed. Chichagov should not have been left so long unaware of Napoleon's change of direction, and that nobody ordered the burning of the Zembin bridges, when they had been prepared with faggots for exactly that purpose, was inexcusable. Napoleon's whole gamble depended upon this escape route. Then there was the dilatoriness of Kutuzov. He failed to coordinate his three armies. He had sent ahead from the Dnieper a small force, but his army of 50,000 played no part in the battle. Wittgenstein and Chichagov arrived too late on each bank to crush the bridgeheads. It is often said that the Beresina was one of Napoleon's greatest feats, and its astonishing success excused the failure of the whole campaign. But he emerged with only half his army intact. It was his own survival, like Ney's on the Dnieper, that has given the battle its immortal celebrity.

CHAPTER EIGHT

HOW IT ENDED

On 29 November 1812 the army began to move over the Zembin causeway, and, when the last of the rearguard was clear, they set fire to the bridges, thus preventing the Russian pursuit by the very method that the Russians could have used to prevent Napoleon's escape. The next stage of the march (160 miles to Vilna) was the worst. The cold suddenly intensified. During October and November the temperature for that time of year had not been abnormal. Except in Smolensk it had seldom dropped below 22° Fahrenheit, and during the three days before the crossing of the Beresina it had risen above freezing-point. But December was one of the coldest on record. Wilson wrote of 'the subtle, keen, razor-cutting, creeping wind that penetrated skin, muscle, bone to the very marrow, rendering the surface as white, and the whole limb affected as fragile, as alabaster. These ravages were terrifically destructive. A general recklessness confounded all ranks, command ceased, and it became a *sauve-qui-peut* at a funeral pace.'

No manoeuvre was possible any more. It was a question of remaining alive and covering the distance. The Russians, except for the Cossacks, more or less abandoned the pursuit. Alexander from St Petersburg was urging them on, but he had no visual evidence (though he might have imagined it) of the condition of the Russian army. Contrary to what is often supposed, the Russian soldiers had no winter clothing, and no natural immunity or skills to protect them against the cold. Kutuzov had a force of about 30,000 men still capable of action, double Napoleon's, but there was no purpose in making another attempt to cut off the French retreat, when cold and starvation would do the work for him.

Different accounts of this march dwell on different aspects of it, according to the writer's desire to emphasize its horrors or the army's heroism. The figures speak for themselves. If 30,000 combatants crossed the Beresina, a week later there were only 13,000 left in a condition to fight, the remainder not all dead, but dying or disarmed and totally downcast. Drowsiness, says Caulaincourt, was a normal reaction to the cold, and usually fatal. 'To sleep is to die.' Mutual help and sympathy became rare luxuries. Nothing makes a man more selfish and pusillanimous than cold. Their only comradeship was in death. When one of Berthier's aides-de-camp was killed, and someone muttered a word of commiseration, Ney retorted, 'Well, it was his turn. Better that we should miss him than he should miss us'; and when a wounded man begged him for help, he replied, 'What do you expect me to do? You're just a casualty of the war.' He believed that it was the destiny of every soldier to die a violent death, and expected to do so himself, and did, but by a firing-squad, inexcusably. Meanwhile, survival depended upon self-interest. If a piece of bread or horseflesh were left unattended for a few seconds, you snatched it.

On the other hand, the men who had crossed the Beresina were the hardiest and had salvaged something of their pride. Mutiny did not occur to them. Even if they had the energy to foment it, there would have been no point in it, because their common cause was to reach Vilna, where there were thought to be abundant supplies. Napoleon rode in his carriage among the rabble, expressing no concern for their distress because it would only have augmented it, and they made no protest, being too proud to complain, and too experienced not to realize its uselessness. They marched in silence, says Ségur, sustained by hope and memories of more fortunate days. The officers were still respected because they shared their men's ordeal. Some order was restored, now that the enemy's pressure was relaxed. The remaining stragglers organized themselves into groups of twenty, with a horse carrying their food, which would itself become food when its load was exhausted. Caulaincourt records that the Guard 'still made an excellent impression by virtue of their general appearance, their vigour, and their martial air. These veterans cheered as soon as they caught sight of the Emperor, and the battalion on guard-duty kept up an astonishing standard of smartness.' He adds that the atmosphere of the headquarters mess was 'generally gay, careless, even full of raillery', as on the day before or after a battle. There comes a moment in bad weather when worse weather becomes slightly comic, and one can boast of it.

Written orders were issued each night for the next day's march, and the precision of them, their formal language, sustained the impression that this was a disciplined army conducting a well-ordered retreat. For example, on 2 December, Berthier (one marvels that his fingers could even hold a pen) wrote to Davout:

L'intention de l'Empereur est que le Vice-Roi [Eugène] cantonne demain ses troupes dans les environs de Molodetchno. L'intention de Sa Majesté est que vous cantonniez également vos troupes dans les environs de cette ville afin que vous ralliez votre Corps et que vous preniez quelques instants de repos.*

Again on 6 December:

Faites mettre en marche demain votre Corps d'Armée à 8 heures et demie précises du matin pour se rendre à Miedniki en suivant le mouvement de la vieille garde, qui partira à 8 heures.†

He gave constant reminders that the army's pay-chests must be guarded, and its remaining trophies. They expected to find rations at Smorgoni. There was not a single note of panic, praise or reproach. Perhaps the most pathetic aspect of these orders was that Berthier should still refer to Davout's '*Corps d'Armée*', when it was reduced to a few hundred men.

At Molodetchno they gained the main road which led from Minsk to Vilna, and there on 3 December Napoleon received

---

* The Emperor's intention is that the Viceroy should make camp tomorrow near Molodetchno, and that you should camp near the same town, so that you can rally your Corps and take a little rest.
† Start your Corps marching at 8.30 am precisely tomorrow in the direction of Miedniki, following the tail of the Old Guard, which will leave at 8 am.

despatches from Paris, among them a letter from Marie-Louise, who, in common with all its citizens, had no conception of the Grand Army's present and past ordeals. Napoleon was pleased by its gentle innocence. 'She is just the woman I needed, kind, good, loving, as German women are. She doesn't busy herself with intrigues. She has a sense of order, and concerns herself only with me and her son.' But he decided that Paris could no longer be kept in ignorance of what was happening, and dictated his famous 29th Bulletin, which told a creditable amount of the truth. It was better that France should hear the worst from him than by rumour. Naturally he played up the successes – Ney's escape and the 'victory' of the Beresina – but he admitted the loss of 30,000 horses (it was far more) and of Partouneaux's division, and emphasized the severity of the climate, even exaggerating its effect before they reached Smolensk:

This army, so splendid on the 6th November, was totally changed by the 14th, with almost no cavalry, no artillery, no transport.... Those men whom Nature had not hardened against all chances of fate and fortune seemed shaken; they lost their cheerfulness and good humour, and saw ahead of them nothing but disaster and catastrophe. Those on whom she had bestowed superior powers kept up their spirits and normal disposition, seeing in the various ordeals a challenge to win new glory.

He ended the despatch with words that seemed to many unforgivably callous: 'His Majesty's health has never been better,' but it was necessary to reassure Paris of this truth. It was rumoured that he was ill or dead.

To Maret in Vilna he gave orders that food should be sent ahead to the army. That their need had not been anticipated is astonishing evidence of the inefficiency of their communications. Now Napoleon's cry for help was unmistakable: 'Food, food, food – without it there are no horrors that this undisciplined mass will not commit in Vilna.' He ordered Maret to rid the town of all foreign agents so that they would not witness and report their arrival: 'The army is not a good sight today.' Perhaps they would make Vilna their winter quarters; or they might not be safe till behind the Niemen.

Meanwhile he had no choice but to force the army to march onwards. As he had few guns left, and little ammunition, and was almost destitute of cavalry, he could not risk another battle. The action was confined to Ney's rearguard. Chichagov's men were beginning to close up, and at Molodetchno, a few hours after Napoleon left it, there was a brisk skirmish which ended in street-fighting and almost the last cannon-fire of the campaign. Victor then took over command of the rearguard, and Ney followed Napoleon into Smorgoni, to hear that he had decided to leave the army and return to Paris.

The Emperor was well aware of the consternation that his departure would cause. To many it seemed like desertion. Once before he had abandoned an army, in Egypt in 1799, and his excuse then had been far more flimsy and had aroused deeper resentment among the 30,000 men left to endure two more years in the Nile valley. At Smorgoni his motives and excuses were more reasonable. When an army is reduced in size to little more than a single corps, it is the accepted practice for the political Head-of-State to order its commander home, as Churchill ordered Gort to return from Dunkirk in 1940. Napoleon was himself head of state, and could not hide behind superior orders, as he had tried to hide behind the Directory in 1799. But the logic of his decision convinced responsible men. The 29th Bulletin was already on its way to Paris. It would cause panic when it was published, being so unexpected, and only the Emperor's presence could restore calm. He could argue, justifiably, that he had surmounted the greatest crisis, the Beresina, and had led his men back from Moscow to the point where they were within reach of safety at Vilna, forty miles away. There was no point in remaining with them just for the sake of sustaining morale, when they were no longer a fighting force. There were experienced subordinates to take his place. He was not like the captain of a sinking ship, the first to take to the boats. He was the Emperor. He must think of his alliances, particularly of Austria and Prussia. He could have no hold upon their loyalty from Vilna. He said to Rapp, 'When they know I am in Paris, leading the nation, they will think twice before raising war against me.'

Only from the Tuileries could he organize the raising of a new army to rescue the old, as he sometimes pretended, but, as there was so little left to rescue, he meant his power and reputation. 'Vilna is well stocked with supplies, and will put everything to rights.... The Russians will be at least as tired as we are, and they are suffering just as much from the cold. They are sure to go into winter quarters. Nothing will be seen of them except the Cossacks.' The piling up of arguments and false hopes betrayed his anxiety that he would be accused of cowardice – which it was not.

The advice he received was not quite unanimous. Daru said that the army would dissolve without him. So did Maret, writing from Vilna. He argued that the Empire would obey his orders as readily if they came from Vilna as from Paris. His departure would confirm that the Russian campaign had been a total failure, and Prussia would be far more likely to defect if he were back in France instead of on the Prussian border. Napoleon replied that to remain with a defeated army would tarnish his glory far more than to leave it.

On the evening of 5 December he summoned his closest associates to tell them that he would be leaving for Paris in a few hours' time. He read them the 29th Bulletin. He again rehearsed the reasons which he had communicated to a few of them a little earlier. The majority urged him to leave. They waited anxiously to hear whom he would take with him, and who would be left in command. All hoped that they might be chosen to accompany him, expressing their devotion to his person and trying to conceal (what must have been very evident) their hope to see their families again and escape this atrocious climate before it grew even worse. He said he would take only Caulaincourt, Duroc, Fain and a few other men of less repute. Berthier protested that he was being separated from the Emperor for the first time in sixteen years, but was ordered to remain with the army, to organize it, so that as little as possible would seem changed after his departure.

As for command, he nominated Murat, because although not so cool a leader as Eugène, he was more inspiring. Later he admitted that the choice was mistaken. In February 1813 he said to Louis Molé, 'Murat lost me my army, because, when I left, I

assumed privileges'. If France did not resist, England would take over all the sea-routes and dominate Europe. So it went on, hour after hour of self-justification, self-delusion, self-aggrandizement.

They halted only to change horses, and snatched a meal whenever they could find a humble inn-keeper to cook it, trusting to the people's ignorance of his features not to recognize him, for although still 'M. de Reyneval' and Caulaincourt ostensibly his master, he was not disguised and could not alter his habitual manner of command. If rumour spread, he would out-distance it.

They reached Warsaw on 10 December. Here all pretence was dropped. Leaving the sleigh at an outer gate, they walked to the central square, where they took rooms at the Hôtel d'Angleterre. The French Ambassador, the Abbé Pradt, Archbishop of Malines, was summoned by Caulaincourt, and arrived astonished to find the Emperor in Warsaw. His first error was to say to Napoleon, 'How are you?' as if man to man. Napoleon ignored this, and began his rehearsed abuse of the Ambassador for the poor contribution Poland had made to the campaign, blaming the Ambassador's indolence. The Abbot then made his second mistake. He defended himself vigorously and impertinently. Why had no Cossacks been raised in Poland? Because there was no money to pay them. After an hour of such argument, Napoleon, who despised non-military men who aired their views on war, scribbled a card to Caulaincourt, 'Get rid of this scoundrel,' by which he meant sack him, but was persuaded that the Ambassador's dismissal would make a poor impression on the Poles, and the card was thrown into the fire. Next he saw Count Taillis, military Governor of Warsaw, and some of the Polish ministers, who escaped more lightly because he could boast to them about his successes in Russia, even claiming that he still had an army of 150,000 in Vilna and would soon replace all his lost equipment. He spoke with gloating pleasure of the new army he would raise, and had barely a word of regret to utter for the one he had just lost. His comment to Caulaincourt was that the Russians should have made a better job of it.

They mounted the sleigh again, and with fresh horses drove west into the night, across a strip of Prussian territory into

Saxony. Momentarily he was tempted to turn off the road to visit Marie Walewska in her chateau of Walewice, but Caulaincourt dissuaded him (in any case Walewska was in Paris at the time), and they passed the weary hours talking politics again. Suddenly Napoleon asked his companion what the Prussians would do if they caught them. Caulaincourt said that they would be killed. But if they were taken alive, mused Napoleon, laughing at the idea, what then? They would be handed over to the English, who would exhibit them in an iron cage in the middle of London, smeared with honey and slowly devoured by flies. The joke lasted almost as far as Dresden.

They arrived there at midnight 13/14 December. Nobody was astir in the bitter weather. They sought the French Minister's house, and drove aimlessly round the streets till they saw a lighted window. The postillion knocked at the door, and a man wearing a night-cap put his head out of the window and asked what they wanted. When they explained that they were expected by the French Minister, the man banged down the window angrily. This was Napoleon's reception in the city which he had entered in such glory six months before. Eventually they found the house, and Napoleon sat down to dictate a dozen letters. He seemed tireless, but not so tireless as Caulaincourt, who had to write them out and despatch them while Napoleon supped and went to sleep. The King of Saxony came at 3 am for a short interview, and at 7 they were off again, this time in the King's more comfortable coach, mounted on runners and equipped with delicacies from the royal kitchens and cellars. They passed through Leipzig, Auerstadt and Erfurt to Frankfurt, and thence across the Rhine at Mainz on 16 December. 'How far to Paris?' asked the Emperor. 'Forty-four hours, Sire.' 'I say thirty-six.' Napoleon's endless stream of reminiscence, speculation and gossip continued. They changed vehicles several times, as one broke, or the snow thinned and runners must be replaced by wheels again, and just beyond Verdun another breakage caused them to transfer into a little open cabriolet, and yet again at Meaux, where they made their final change into the postmaster's post-chaise, a cumbersome carriage with two enormous wheels; and it was in this ungainly vehicle that the Emperor entered Paris just before midnight on 18 December.

They drove straight to the Tuileries. Caulaincourt ends this part of the story:

I had unbuttoned my overcoat in such a manner as to display the facings of my uniform. Taking us for officers bearing despatches, the sentries let us pass and we made our way to the entrance of the gallery that opens on to the garden. The Swiss porter had gone to bed, but, lamp in hand and dressed only in his shirt, he came to see who was knocking. We cut such odd figures that he summoned his wife. I had to assert my identity several times before either of them could be persuaded to open the door, for it was not without considerable difficulty and much rubbing of eyes that he and his wife, who held the lamp beneath my very nose, were eventually able to recognize me. The woman opened the door while he went off to summon one of the footmen on duty. The Empress had only just gone to bed. In pursuance of the plan we had agreed upon, I caused myself to be conducted to the apartments of her ladies-in-waiting, ostensibly with news of the Emperor, who was supposed to be following after me. While these various confabulations were going on, the Swiss, and several others who were gathered round, were eyeing His Majesty from head to foot. Suddenly one of them cried: "It is the Emperor!"

Their delight was indescribable. They could not contain themselves for joy. The Empress's two waiting women were coming out of her room at the very moment that I was shown into theirs. My fortnight's growth of beard, my dress and heavy fur-lined boots created no better impression here than they had done on the Swiss, for I had to insist that I was the bearer of good news from the Emperor before I could prevent them running away for safety from the spectre-like creature before them. Mention of the Emperor's name at last served to reassure them and assist their recognition of me. One of them went to announce me to Her Majesty.

In the meantime the Emperor, who was barely able to conceal his impatience, brought my embassy to an abrupt end by going in to the Empress without further ado, remarking, 'Goodnight, Caulaincourt. Like me you are in need of rest.'

Caulaincourt admitted he was. He had not shut his eyes for fourteen days and nights, and after reaching Paris it was another fortnight before he could sleep properly. The only other physical effect of the journey was 'a certain thinness'.

Amazingly, for they had been 'speeding on like travellers through the infernal regions', couriers had caught up with them on the road, having left Vilna a day after them. The news was bad. Murat and Berthier reported that the rout continued. The deepening cold had caused many to desert the colours, even some of the Guard, on whom Napoleon's departure had had a most depressing effect. Belief in his genius had given them confidence, fear of his scorn had commanded their obedience. Now he was gone. He had been the fount of all orders, and they would not give their allegiance to any other. On 11 December Murat admitted that he had lost control. 'Every human effort is hopeless to remedy the disorder. One can only resign oneself.' On the next day, only a week after Napoleon's departure, Berthier confirmed, 'The whole army is completely disbanded, even the Guard, which has only 4–500 men left.... The army no longer exists.' Napoleon's replies, delayed a month or more, were totally without sympathy. 'A captain of light infantry', he said to Caulaincourt, 'could have commanded the army better than Murat,' and on 26 January 1813 he wrote to Murat a letter of cruel reprimand: 'I am not going to tell you how displeased I am with your conduct,' he began, and then proceeded to do exactly that: 'It has been diametrically opposed to your duties. It is due to your weak character, as usual. You are a good soldier on the battlefield, but off it you have no energy, and no character.... The title of King has turned your head. If you want to keep it, behave yourself, and be careful what you say.' The latter warning must have been caused by some exasperated words which Murat let fall to Davout, who reported them: 'One can no longer serve such a maniac. Nobody can believe in his promises or treaties. Napoleon was a fool not to have treated with the English,' and so on in increasingly vituperative language, provoking Davout to protest that Murat's outburst was base ingratitude. He owed everything to Napoleon. It was scarcely surprising that by then the decencies of ordinary intercourse between generals had been forgotten. Their sufferings were acute.

The coldest day of the winter was 6 December, when the temperature fell to −36° Fahrenheit. Across the melancholy landscape crawled a long column of unhappy men, dull-eyed, their faces ravaged by smoke and cold. A high wind whipped the snow into a blizzard, even when no fresh snow was falling, and exposed the underlying sheet-ice on the road, making movement on foot or hoof all but impossible. A fallen man rarely rose again, and he was stripped of his warm clothing before he died. Ségur, now attached to Murat's headquarters, wrote that he walked thirty miles carrying 75 lbs of personal equipment. He tried to mount a horse. It collapsed on top of him. Several hundred men passed before one stopped to help him. He had nothing to eat all day. That night he tried to sleep in a hut surrounded by corpses. Next to it was a large barn in which 400 men huddled round a fire. At least three-quarters of them froze to death during the night, the dying clambering over the dead to reach the warmth. Those who succeeded found that the heat turned their frozen limbs gangrenous, and the only cure for gangrene was amputation, for which there were no surgeons or instruments. Soldiers would set whole houses on fire and stand around them all night, and they ate horse-flesh, rye seasoned with cartridge-powder, or each other. Stendhal records the terrible sight of men drinking their own blood, eating their own severed fingers. Fezensac gives this scene:

The road was covered with Russian prisoners whom we didn't guard any more. Some dragged themselves along mechanically, on bare and frost-bitten feet. Others had fallen into a sort of savage stupidity.... Those too feeble to fetch wood stopped near the first fire they came across, and sat on top of each other to receive its warmth, and when the fire died, so did they.

And from the other side, Sir Robert Wilson:

During these last marches, the Russian troops, who were moving through a country devastated by the enemy, suffered nearly as much as they did from want of fuel, food and clothing. The soldier had no additional covering for the night's bivouac on the frozen snow, and to sleep longer than half-an-hour at a time was probable death. Officers and men were therefore obliged to relieve each other in their snatches of sleep, and to force up the reluctant and frequently resisting slumberers. Firing could scarcely ever be obtained, and when obtained, the fire could only be approached with very great caution, as it caused gangrene in the frozen parts. But as water itself froze at only 3 ft from the largest fire, it was almost necessary to burn before the sensation of heat could be felt. About 90,000 perished, and of the 10,000 recruits who afterwards marched on Vilna as reinforcements, only 1,500 reached the city, and the greater part of these were conveyed to the hospitals as sick or mutilated.

In the Grand Army, about another 20,000 dropped away between Smorgoni and Vilna, and these included men of Loison's division sent forward from the town to reinforce and hearten the survivors of the Beresina, but, coming from relatively comfortable billets, they were less prepared for the agony of the march and were infected by the moral and physical degeneration of those whom they joined. The army came to Vilna on 8 December as a rabble, pushing each other aside at the bridges and defiles, the horses held up by the shafts more than straining to pull them, not a single cavalryman mounted, not a soldier capable of fighting on either side except the Cossacks, who swarmed around them day and night.

Vilna was the first sizeable town they had entered since Smolensk, and it was well stocked. There was flour and meat to feed 100,000 men for forty days. Preparations had been made to receive an orderly force. But as there was no organization among the arriving troops, there could be no organized system of billeting or food distribution. To say that they assaulted Vilna would not be an overstatement. The famished men forced their way into the town, all by the same gate, neglecting the others because to reach them would add another mile to the intolerable march. They invaded the warehouses and private houses, fighting for food and drink, over-eating and over-drinking, wasting much of it, overlooking great quantities because they were in no mood to listen to directions. The terrified population barricaded the doors of their shops and houses, as much from fear of Russian reprisals if they helped the French as of the plunderers themselves. Vilna, before the arrival of the army, had had the appearance of a normal provincial capital. It was unburnt, and the people went about their ordinary business. Now suddenly no private property was sacred, every man seeking a well-heated room, a well-stocked larder, and, because nearly all of them were in need of medical help, they crowded into the hospitals, which were already filled with the wounded of the earlier part of the campaign. This is what Wilson found a few days later:

> The hospital of St Bazile presented the most awful and hideous sight. 7,500 bodies were piled like pigs of lead over one another in the corridors; carcasses were strewn about in every part; and all the broken windows and walls were stuffed with feet, legs, arms, hands, trunks and heads to fit the apertures and keep out the cold air from the living. The putrefaction of thawing flesh emitted the most cadaverous smell.

As the army was totally out of control, except for a few hundreds in the Guard, they could not be assembled to meet the Cossack threat. The remnants of Loison's and Wrede's division undertook the task, but uselessly. The Cossacks came up to the outskirts, grew bolder as they encountered little opposition, and a few galloped into the streets, to be welcomed by the population. Murat ordered a general evacuation only twenty-four hours after their arrival, although Napoleon's orders had been specific: they must hold Vilna for at least eight days to give the army time to recuperate.

Somehow, about 10,000 men resumed the march on 10 December. Many others ignored the order, preferring capture, or never received it. Three miles outside the town they came to an ice-bound hill called Ponarskaia which proved unsurmountable by horses dragging heavy loads. Nobody thought of seeking side-roads, which did exist, to bypass the hill. It was the culmination of all their sufferings. For several hours (Ségur says fifteen) they struggled against the slope. 'The drivers whipped and swore at their horses,' wrote Thiers, 'but finding no foothold on the ice, fell bleeding to their knees, while the cannon, abandoned halfway up the hill, rolled back, crushing everyone in their path.' Ultimately they were obliged to leave at the foot of the hill all the carts and wounded, and the rearguard pillaged the army's pay-chests rather than leave them to the Russians, but such was the state of disorder that the Cossacks saw no point in further massacre, and began to loot the waggons alongside the French.

They continued the last seventy miles to Kovno, stupefied by cold and misery; the eagles, saved from the wreckage, were almost the only remaining evidence of their pride. It was like a descent, infinitely magnified, from an unsuccessful attempt on a Himalayan peak. There was one last flurry of resistance, organized by Ney, who once again commanded the rearguard. Kovno lies on the east bank of the Niemen; the bridge was beyond it. As the river was frozen solid, and could be crossed at almost any point on foot, the bridge was no longer essential to either side, but instinctively they regarded it as a last outpost. Nay defended the town for a night and a day (13/14 December) with its garrison of 300 Prussians, whom he found equipped with a few cannon. They were indifferent troops. The gunners fled as the Cossacks approached, spiking their guns, and when the Prussian officer was wounded in the thigh, he put a bullet through his head, fearing torture if he were captured. His men deserted, but Ney, seizing a rifle, rallied a handful. He held the Vilna gate till nightfall, and then withdrew across the Niemen, burning the bridge behind him. He was the last man of the Grand Army to leave the soil of Russia. Such was the indomitable spirit of a very rare man.

Murat gave orders that the army should disperse among the fortress towns of Prussia and the Grand Duchy of Warsaw. The majority found their way to Gumbinnen and Königsberg, and from there in early January to Danzig, Berlin, Warsaw and Posen, where Murat left them (*'ce n'est pas un climat pour un Roi de Naples'*) to return to Italy, handing over his command to Eugène. On their march through Prussia they were spared pursuit by the Russians, who halted temporarily at their frontier, and were treated with generous kindliness by many of the inhabitants. The 29th Bulletin had been widely circulated. Hatred had given place to pity, and enquiries as to what had befallen them were more compassionate than malicious. Count Dumas, the Intendant-General, had found lodgings in a doctor's house at Gumbinnen. 'We had just been served some excellent coffee when I saw a man in a brown coat come in. He had a long beard. His face was black and seemed to be burnt. His eyes were red and glistening. "Here I am at last," he said.' Dumas failed to recognize him. It was Ney. After firing his last shot, and throwing his weapon into the Niemen, he had escaped alone through the woods.

One formation of Napoleon's army had a different experience, Macdonald's Tenth Corps, which had been isolated on the left wing since the campaign began. It had not earned much glory, but it had remained more or less intact. After retreating from the siege of Riga, and left almost without orders, Macdonald withdrew to Tilsit in mid-December. His rearguard, commanded by General Yorck with 17,000 Prussians and sixty guns, was surrounded by the Russians, and on 30 December Yorck agreed, without permission, to become 'neutral', by signing the Convention of Tauroggen. It was a euphemism for surrender or desertion. The King of Prussia at first disowned the Convention, but later accepted it. The force was allowed to withdraw to Memel on condition that they did not resume active operations against the Russians for two months. Macdonald found his way through Tilsit to Königsberg in early January, and his 7,000 men were incorporated with the other relics of the Grand Army. In the far south Schwarzenberg (Austrian) and Reynier (Saxon) retreated in their own time across their frontiers, almost intact.

How many, then, survived the Russian campaign? It is difficult to be precise, as contemporary records were either lost or were inevitably inexact. There is also the complication that many thousands joined the army as reinforcements during the campaign, others were detached to the flanks or rear, and a surprising number (30,000, says Seton-Watson) eventually regained western Europe from Russian captivity during the next two years. It is certain that half a million crossed the Niemen in June 1812, and, adding the reinforcements, let us say that 5,000 re-crossed it in organized units in December, and another 25,000 as stragglers. No estimate has ever been made of the number of civilians who survived, like Louise Fusil. Macdonald brought out another 7,000, and Schwarzenberg and Reynier perhaps 35,000. Chandler (in his *The Campaigns of Napoleon*) sums up: 'In round figures Napoleon lost 570,000 soldiers. Of these perhaps 370,000 died on the battlefield, of illness or exposure. The remaining 200,000 fell into Russian hands.' In addition, says Chandler, he lost over 200,000 trained horses, and at least 1,000 guns. A few figures can be added from other sources to illustrate what these losses meant to individual formations and units. The Guard, which set off 47,000 strong, returned with little over 1,500, although they had not been involved in heavy fighting. The 6th Regiment of Tirailleurs left Smolensk during the retreat with thirty-one officers and three hundred other ranks: at the Niemen they had fourteen officers and ten men. For Fezensac's 4th Regiment in Ney's corps we have more detailed figures. They crossed the Rhine in May with 2,150 men; 400 reinforcements joined them at Moscow, another 400 at Smolensk, and 50 at Vilna. Of this total of 3,000, only 300 survived the campaign, 100 of them as returned prisoners-of-war.

In comparison with later wars, the officers came off better than their men. This was certainly not due to shirking their duty in battle, but their hardships on the march were a little alleviated by being mounted until the last stages, by having the money to buy furs and food when they were available, and by the care taken of them by their personal servants. It is noteworthy that all the most senior officers escaped with their lives – Napoleon, Berthier, Davout, Murat, Ney, Eugène, Oudinot, St Cyr, Bessières, Grouchy, Poniatowski, Macdonald and Schwarzenberg. The most serious loss was the engineer Eblé, the hero of the Beresina, who died at Königsberg before the end of the year as a direct result of his ordeal.

The Russian losses are estimated by Chandler to have been 150,000 who died from all causes, 'and at least twice as many more must have been crippled by wounds or frostbite. An incalculable number of Russian civilians must also have suffered during the seven months of bitter fighting.'

CHAPTER NINE

WHY NAPOLEON FAILED

Thiers wrote, 'Nothing, or almost nothing, could have made the expedition succeed.' The same could be said about almost every successful campaign in history, like Alexander the Great's conquest of Persia or Washington's continued defiance of the British after Valley Forge, when the odds against success were even greater than Napoleon's. The causes of his failure in Russia are not only evident to us now, but could have been foreseen by the greatest of generals in time to avoid them. His error was not, as he later maintained, that he tried to do in one year what should have taken two, but in six months what should have taken four.

Let us imagine with hindsight how it might have gone, given that the campaign was necessary at all. He assembles an army not of 675,000 men but of 300,000, mainly French, and concentrates them on a narrow front, as he did his main force on the Niemen. He ignores his flanks, except by inviting the Prussians to defend Prussia, the Poles their duchy and the Austrians Austria, by stationing their regular armies on their frontiers with Russia, in defensive positions, allied but not belligerent. He declares the independence of Poland, and guarantees Austria against any threat to them from the north. He announces that he will free the Russian serfs. He advances in May across the Niemen to seize the Vitebsk–Orsha gap, moving so fast between Barclay's and Bagration's armies that he prevents them from joining, throwing one back against the Baltic, the other against the Pripet marsh, and captures Smolensk. There he pauses, for three reasons: to rest the Grand Army; to move up his main supplies to Smolensk; and to defeat each Russian army in detail as they attempt to move up ahead of or behind him. He continues almost unopposed to Moscow, offers peace to the Tsar, and if it is refused (it is now only August), he detaches half his force to capture St Petersburg, and with the other half occupies Tula and Kaluga, the main Russian bases. Russia is left without either of her capitals, without an army, without supplies, and without the support of ninety per cent of her people, the serfs. From Alexander all he demands is the full re-imposition of the Continental System and a new alliance, like Tilsit's. Jointly they could conquer Constantinople. He then withdraws from Russia before the winter, leaving a considerable army on the Niemen to threaten a repetition of the campaign if the Tsar defaults.

Such a strategy (which is introduced here only as an historical war-game) might have succeeded. Instead, what happened? Napoleon decided that because the country was so vast, a vast army was needed to conquer it. Because the best of his French troops were engaged in Spain, he must enrol troops from his subject nations, whose reliability was dependent upon his continued success. In this he was more fortunate than he deserved. The Poles fought brilliantly at Borodino, the Italians at Maloyaroslavets, and Victor's mixed corps at the Beresina. But there was a wastefulness in the multi-national composition of the Grand Army, in its wide deployment, and particularly in its size. The army was too large and too broadly dispersed for one man to control it over such great distances. The two wings were like thalidomide limbs, feeble and ineffectual, and, instead of sustaining the main effort, they weakened it. The very fact that both survived almost intact is proof of the poor contribution they made to it. The Turkish peace and Swedish neutrality had freed two Russian armies unexpectedly. Macdonald could not prevent Wittgenstein from moving south, nor could Schwarzenberg prevent Chichagov from moving north, to intercept Napoleon's retreat. The first never captured Riga, the second lost Minsk, because neither had their hearts in the campaign. The Poles were never given their promised independence for fear of alienating Austria. The serfs were never offered the hope of emancipation, owing to Napoleon's reluctance to betray the Russian and Polish aristocracy.

At the centre, the campaign started a month too late, like Hitler's. There were inexcusable delays of eighteen days at Vilna and twelve at Vitebsk, when speed of movement was the key to the defeat of the two widely separated Russian armies, which lacked central control. Too much reliance was placed upon living off the country, when Napoleon had been warned of Russian scorched-earth. Too little forethought was given to the difficulty of moving supplies forward along indifferent roads. The main depots were located too far back, at Danzig and Königsberg, and the advanced depots were insufficiently guarded: at Vitebsk and Minsk vast stores fell easily into Russian hands. Provisions for the horses, which were even more essential than the men, were wholly inadequate. They carried the stores, drew the guns and mounted the cavalry, Napoleon's main protection against the Cossacks. The cumulative result was that more men were lost during the advance to Moscow than on the retreat from it, and they were not mainly battle casualties, but losses by starvation, exhaustion, sickness, capture and desertion.

The legend propagated by Napoleon in his 29th Bulletin and ever afterwards was that he was defeated by the cold. In his address to the Senate, two days after returning to Paris, he said, 'My army has had some losses, but this was due to the premature vigour of the season.' How then could he explain that he crossed the Niemen with half a million men and arrived in Moscow with only 100,000? The others were not, in the main, battle-casualties or left behind to guard his communications, but victims of the debilitating summer, poor logistics, and the shocking inadequacy of the medical services. During the retreat he lost fewer men, because there were fewer men to lose. The winter, as far as the Beresina, was exceptionally mild, but it seemed more severe because no preparations had been made to meet it. The whole campaign was wrecked by Napoleon's optimism that it would not be so hot on the way out, nor so cold in the closing stages on the way back, and that the initiative and endurance of his men would somehow enable them to survive.

The battle of Borodino and the burning of Moscow were in no sense decisive. The first did not win or lose the campaign (it might have been won if he had agreed to use the Guard), and the second did not make his retreat inevitable. But because the

battle resulted in Kutuzov surrendering Moscow, and the fire
was followed by Napoleon's retreat, both seemed at the time
climacteric events. Kutuzov could have fought a second battle to
defend Moscow, as the Russians did successfully in 1941. Napoleon could have remained there for the entire winter. He was
probably right to leave the city, but although he blamed himself
afterwards for the delay in doing so, it was understandable. To
retreat was an admission of failure, and the decision demanded
much moral courage. It was not impossible that Alexander would
sue for peace, given the political and military tradition of the
times. Napoleon had in mind not a retreat, but a further advance,
southwards, to meet and defeat Kutuzov. After Maloyaroslavets
his strategy faltered. Then there was no strategy except escape.
So he was committed to a retreat in mid-winter, abandoning all
his gains, all his trophies, even his bridging-team at Orsha, and
eventually his army. There were moments of glory – Krasnoe,
the Beresina – but it was a process of mounting wastage and
humiliation. Undoubtedly it represented a failure of imagination
and will.

At forty-two a man's failure can seldom be attributed to his
declining intellectual power, but Napoleon did privately consider
that this might have been a contributory cause. In January 1813,
as he leant against a billiard-table and idly fingered the balls, he
said to Louis Molé, 'It's odd that one's will diminishes while
one's strength survives. When, before, I'd say, Bring me a glass
of lemonade, now I say, Bring me coffee or wine. After thirty
one is no longer so prepared to make war. Alexander the Great
died before this happened.' (Not exactly: Alexander died at
thirty-three). In 1812 Napoleon did from time to time exhibit a
certain mental stodginess, uncharacteristic of his youth. His most
ambitious campaign coincided with a sudden drop in his ability.
His delays and hesitations at Vilna, Vitebsk, Smolensk and Moscow; his unimaginative tactics at Borodino and his avoidance of
the heat of the battle; his failure to limit the baggage on leaving
Moscow; his strategic indecision after Maloyaroslavets; his reluctance to associate himself intimately with the suffering of his
troops during the retreat: all this illustrates his drooping vitality.
Only twice during the campaign did he display the courage and
initiative for which he was renowned: when he was nearly

captured at Ghorodnia, and at the Beresina, but neither incident was comparable to his resilience at Marengo or Wagram. He felt continuously responsible, but now more for his reputation than for his army. The two had ceased to be synonymous. He pretended indifference to his losses. Talking to Metternich in May 1813, he uttered the dreadful verdict: 'A man such as I am does not concern himself much about the lives of a million men.' And then he added: 'The French cannot complain much of me. To spare them, I have sacrificed the Germans and the Poles. I have lost in the campaign of Moscow 300,000 men, and there were not more than 30,000 Frenchmen among them.' His statistics were as false as his morality. Metternich replied, 'You forget, Sire, that you are speaking to a German.'

One should ultimately attribute the catastrophe to his insensate ambition, to what Southey had in mind in calling him,

> Bold man and bad,
> Remorseless, godless, full of fraud and lies,
> And black with murders and with perjuries,

and in appealing to Frenchmen to redeem the dishonour in which he had involved them:

> France, if thou lovest thy ancient fame,
> Revenge thy sufferings and thy shame! ...
> By the flesh that gorged the wolves of Spain,
> Or stiffened on the snowy plain
> Of frozen Muscovy.

Of course Southey was writing as Poet Laureate, before Waterloo, and he was writing about his country's enemy, indifferent to Napoleon's achievement in destroying the injustices of the old régime throughout much of Europe. But Napoleon, like Hitler, persuaded himself that, in attempting to conquer Russia, he was defending Europe against a barbarian threat. Let us consider what he wrote at St Helena in justification of it:

> The Russian war should have been the most popular war of modern times. It was a war on the side of good sense and

sound interests, to bring peace and security to all. It was purely pacific and conservative. It was a war for a great cause, the end of uncertainties, and the beginning of security. A new horizon, and new labours would have opened up, full of well-being and prosperity for all. The European system was established: all that remained was to organize it.... In this way Europe would have become in reality but a single people, and every man travelling anywhere would have found himself in a common fatherland.... Paris would have become the capital of the world and the French the envy of the nations.

Such pleading is intolerable. Let a Frenchman reply. Thiers considered that the whole campaign was unnecessary. If Napoleon had concentrated on winning in Spain, and made a few compromises in eastern Europe, he could have had peace without attacking Russia. There was no intelligible motive for the campaign: he never even bothered to explain it. If Russia had joined England, and Napoleon had waited on the Vistula for Russia to attack, he would have had all Europe on his side. As it was, he ignored the resentment he had aroused by his previous actions. His allies were not allies. They were subject peoples, hoping for his failure. They were obliged to support a campaign of which the main purpose was to sustain an economic strategy from which they were themselves the main sufferers. They had no quarrel with England. He humiliated them by taking their collaboration for granted, and by his extravagant display of his power over them at Dresden. He no longer seemed the liberator of nations, but their oppressor. He was the enemy of the entire world. Even the United States, fighting against England, considered him a tyrant.

What of Russia? There was no question what her attitude would be, for she was the victim of Napoleon's attack, and the whole nation was united in resisting it. But, for so defiant a people, their tactics were strange. They withdrew, and surrendered Moscow. It cannot be considered a deliberate strategy, for they tried to halt Napoleon on the Dvina, then at Smolensk, then at Borodino. It developed out of their failure. It was not preconceived. Kutuzov used time, space and the climate as his allies to exhaust Napoleon as an alternative to defeating him in battle, but only after failing to defeat him. The parallel with the tactics of the Roman General Fabius against Hannibal is so remarkable that Kutuzov must have studied them, and Plutarch's description is worth quoting:

> He did not purpose to fight out the issue with him, but wished, having plenty of time, money and men, to wear out and gradually consume his vigour, his scanty resources and his small army. Therefore he hung threatening over them. If they sat still, he too kept quiet; but if they moved, he would show himself just far enough away to avoid being forced to fight against his will, and yet near enough to make his very delays inspire the enemy with the fear that he was going to give battle at last. But for merely consuming time in this way he was greatly despised by his countrymen and roundly abused even in his own camp.

Kutuzov was not Fabius, but he succeeded by the same methods. Seeing Napoleon in retreat, he guessed that he would not halt this side of Russia's frontier. He used his two other armies, Wittgenstein's and Chichagov's, less as converging jaws to trap Napoleon than as thumb and forefinger on a tube to extrude him. His refusal to employ his entire strength at Krasnoe was a more striking illustration of his method than his inefficient coordination of the three armies at the Beresina. Afterwards, there was no purpose in using his marginal advantage to accomplish what cold, famine and exhaustion would do for him. But he did let a great opportunity slip. Bennigsen wrote, 'It is indisputable that the Grand Army was lost more owing to Napoleon's errors than to Russian resistance.' Kutuzov allowed Napoleon to escape, and his army to claim that they never surrendered. For this the Tsar never forgave him. He said to Sir Robert Wilson at Vilna that he was obliged to reward Kutuzov with the title of Prince of Smolensk, but 'I knew he had done nothing that he ought to have done, nothing against the enemy that he could avoid. All his successes have been forced upon him.' But Alexander well knew that, since the first month of the campaign, he had not been its hero – Kutuzov was. When the Tsar replaced him as Commander-in-Chief in April by Wittgenstein, nobody was greatly surprised. Kutuzov's task was over. A few weeks later he died in Silesia.

Correlli Barnett sums up well the long-term effect of the campaign upon Napoleon's fortunes: 'He had lost more than the greatest of all his campaigns, more than the largest army he was ever to command: he had lost the essential stock-in-trade of a speculator such as he – his credit.'

At first the drama of his sudden re-appearance in Paris minimized the impact of the 29th Bulletin, which had been published two days before his arrival. People talked only of his rapid journey (from Dresden in four days!), and were so pleased to see him, so greatly heartened by his apparent energy (he worked fifteen hours in the Tuileries on the very next day), that only gradually, when news of individual deaths threw a cloud of gloom over Society, did they begin to realize the extent of the disaster and question whether it had all been necessary. Then the lavish receptions and balls which Napoleon staged to restore public spirits and morale seemed an insult to their grief. 'I felt I was dancing on tombs,' said Fezensac, who returned to Paris in time to attend one of them.

The effect of Napoleon's defeat on his allies and subjects was more catastrophic and lasting, but it took a little time to develop. On paper, and on the map, his position at the beginning of 1813 did not look too bad. He was still master of Germany, the Netherlands and Italy. He had formidable garrisons on the Vistula, the Oder and the Elbe. Austria was still his ally. Russia was exhausted and seemed unlikely to make war beyond her frontiers. England, it was true, was winning victories in Spain, but they seemed to Napoleon puny irritations compared to the new strategic moves he was planning. With extraordinary energy he raised a fresh army, calling up young recruits ahead of their year, veterans from their retirement and even sailors from their ships to swell his battalions. The industries of France restored his artillery and his supplies. By April 1813 he could put 200,000 men into the field without touching his divisions in Spain. The only arm in which he was deficient was cavalry, and horses to pull the transports and the guns. It seems incredible that within a year his whole Empire would crumble and he himself be forced into exile.

He failed to foresee that his Russian campaign had so weakened the legend of his invincibility that all the animosity he had aroused in eastern Europe suddenly surfaced. It began in Prussia. The nationalist movement which had been fomenting during 1812 forced its weak king, Frederick-William III, first to endorse Yorck's defection, then to conclude in late February a secret treaty with the Tsar, and two weeks later openly to declare war against France. Secondly, Napoleon had not reckoned with the Tsar's determination that the campaign was not yet over. Having played a minor part since Moscow, Alexander, against the advice of Kutuzov and his other senior commanders, and without the support of the majority of his people, now proclaimed a war of liberation in alliance with Prussia. He forced Eugène to retreat from one river-line to the next: Berlin, Hamburg, Dresden were each given up in turn. Danzig was besieged. Reversing their roles, Eugène could only save his thinly spread army by avoiding battle, hoping to hold a defensive screen long enough for Napoleon to assemble his new army on the Rhine.

He succeeded in doing so, and Napoleon, now numerically stronger, took the offensive to regain what he had lost. He won decisive victories over the Russians and Prussians at Lützen (2 May) and Bautzen (21 May). He then unaccountably accepted an armistice, Metternich acting as his intermediary. At St Helena he said that this armistice was 'the greatest error of my life', but he had said that about other incidents, like remaining too long in Moscow. His reason was that the campaign had revealed to him the inexperience of his new troops. He met Metternich near Dresden. He boasted that his strength and reputation were now fully restored. He spoke of the Russian campaign as if it had been just an accident. The Austrian statesman replied (but we have only his word for it), 'I have seen your soldiers. They are no more than children. And when these infants have been wiped out, what will you have left?' Napoleon, in a rage, refused to convert the armistice into a truce, a truce into a peace conference, a conference into a permanent peace, all of which Metternich offered him, but on conditions which meant that France must relax her hold on eastern Europe. Napoleon refused to surrender a single one of his conquests. On 12 August 1813 Austria declared war on France. The three powers – Austria, Russia and Prussia – joined forces to inflict on Napoleon a major defeat at the battle of Leipzig in mid-October, and the crumbling process began, ending with the Allies' entry into Paris on 31 March 1814, and Napoleon's abdication twelve days later, deserted by his senate and his marshals. Two of them, Murat and Bernadotte, had already joined his enemies.

Thus, while it cannot be said that Napoleon's fall was made inevitable by his retreat from Moscow, it was certainly hastened by it. If his Russian campaign had succeeded, what would have happened? Napoleon's own version at St Helena was that he would have spent a happy old age in company with the Empress, and during the royal apprenticeship of his young son, 'visiting in leisurely fashion, with our own horses like a genuine country couple, every corner of the Empire, receiving complaints, redressing wrongs, and scattering public buildings and benefactions wherever we went'.

History records no example of such an apotheosis for the conqueror of equal nations. A new Coalition would soon have been formed, with England at its head, and perhaps the United States its ally, and there would have been many more years of war until Europe had overthrown the tyrant. An Empire composed of peoples still proud, though subjugated, who possess the ability and strength of will to raise armies and collaborate with each other, and will not desist until they have won back their freedom, is the most fragile of all human institutions.

BIBLIOGRAPHICAL NOTE

The French accounts of the campaign on which I have chiefly relied are:

Caulaincourt, General de, Duke of Vicenza, *Memoirs*, ed. by Jean Hanoteau, translated by Hamish Miles (London, 1935)

Ségur, General Comte de, *La campagne en Russie* (Paris, 1825)

Chambray, Marquis de, *Histoire de l'expédition de Russie* (Paris, 1859)

Chuquet, Arthur, *1812: La guerre en Russie* (Paris, 1912)

Thiers, Louis Adolphe, *The Moscow Expedition*, extracted from Thiers's *Histoire du Consulat et de l'Empire*, ed. with notes by Hereford B. George (Oxford, 1904)

Fezensac, R. E. P. de, *Journal de la campagne de Russie en 1812* (Paris, 1850)

Boutourlin, D. P., *Histoire militaire de la campagne de Russie en 1812* (Paris, 1824)

Bertin, Georges, *La campagne de 1812 d'après des témoins oculaires* (Paris, 1895)

Fusil, Louise, *Souvenir d'une femme sur la retraite de Russie* (Paris, 1910)

From the Russian side I have found most useful:

Bennigsen, General Levin, *Mémoires* (Paris, 1908)

Wilson, Sir Robert, *Journals 1812-14*, ed. by Anthony Brett-James (London, 1964)

Tarlé, Eugène, *Napoleon's Invasion of Russia*, translated by
G. M. (London, 1942)

Clausewitz, Karl von, *Campaign of 1812 in Russia* (London,
1943)

Tolstoy, Leo, *War and Peace*, translated by Rosemary
Edmonds (London, 1957)

Berlin, Sir Isaiah, *The Hedgehog and the Fox* (London, 1953)

Kelly, Laurence, *Moscow, A Travellers' Companion* (London,
1983)

Of British accounts, the best and most recent is:

Palmer, Alan, *Napoleon in Russia* (London, 1967)

Also invaluable:

Chandler, David, *The Campaigns of Napoleon* (London,
1966) and his *Dictionary of the Napoleonic Wars* (London,
1979)

Barnett, Correlli, *Bonaparte* (London, 1976)

Brett-James, Anthony, *Eyewitness Accounts of Napoleon's
Defeat in Russia* (London, 1967)

Cronin, Vincent, *Napoleon* (London, 1971)

Burton, Col. R. C., *Napoleon's Invasion of Russia* (London,
1914)

Macdonnell, A. G., *Napoleon and his Marshals* (London,
1934)

Belloc, Hilaire, *The Campaign of 1812 and the Retreat from
Moscow* (London, 1924)

Seton-Watson, Hugh, *The Russian Empire 1801–1917*
(Oxford, 1967)

Thompson, J. M., *Letters of Napoleon* (Oxford, 1934)

Erickson, John, *The Road to Stalingrad* (London, 1975)

Cecil, Algernon, *Metternich* (London, 1933)

Cooper, Duff, *Talleyrand* (London, 1932)

INDEX